The Celluloid Literature

The Celluloid Literature:
film in the humanities

William Jinks

Miami-Dade Junior College

GLENCOE PRESS
A Division of The Macmillan Company
Beverly Hills, California
Collier-Macmillan Ltd., London

Glencoe Press
A Division of The Macmillan Company
8701 Wilshire Boulevard
Beverly Hills, California 90211
Collier-Macmillan Canada, Ltd., Toronto, Canada

Library of Congress catalog card number 79-123450

First printing, 1971

To Sandy

Contents

Introduction

ARRIVING when it did on the very eve of the twentieth century, the film offered the storyteller an entirely new means of shaping a work of fiction. Like the novel, an older narrative predecessor, film soon learned to incorporate and absorb what it needed from other arts. Music, for example, provided it with a model for rhythm and counterpoint and, from theater, film acquired an understanding of the nature of spectacle, but it was with the literary form that the film shared and continues to share the greatest number of affinities.

Superficially film appears to resemble a kind of "canned theater," and although its means of representation is visual, its method of artistic control is actually very close to that of the novel's. For example, a film maker, like a novelist, can instantly shift our attention from a vast panorama to the most minute detail because, in the film, our attention is not free to wander as it is in the theater. In addition, it is clear that the film maker, unlike the dramatist, is not confined to the physical limitations of the stage.

The film, however, did indeed draw from the theater as it did from the novel, and since the narrative film was able to emulate and to learn from the older narrative arts, it attained artistic maturity in a short period of time. As French film critic André Bazin once suggested, "It may be that the past 20 years in the cinema will be reckoned in its overall history as the equivalent of five centuries in literature." Bazin's remarks make us realize that today's film is a relatively mature art form.

It is difficult, for example, to ignore the fact that many of the outstanding narratives of the twentieth century have been films. Film makers such as Chaplin, Eisenstein, Renoir, Welles, Bresson, Antonioni, Bergman, Fellini, and Resnais have bequeathed us a body of work whose significance is only now beginning to be understood. In addition to its own legacy, the film has been a direct influence on contemporary fiction as well. Its impact on the work of John Dos Passos, William Burroughs, and Alain Robbe-Grillet, to name only a few writers, has been fairly well established.

But, even more importantly, the filmed narrative has permanently altered the way in which we respond to fiction. Stylistic techniques that originated in film, such as the flashback, the dissolve, slow motion, and montage have slowly found their way into the novel and the short story. Under the influence of film, the often ornate rhetoric of the 18th and 19th century has given way to the terse "realistic" dialogue of the 20th century. In addition, the camera's singularly objective manner of narrating a story has given rise to a point of view that is often described as the "fly-on-the-wall" or "the camera" point of view. Thus, the film has not only influenced the existing modes of fiction but it has extended them by offering the storyteller an alternative means of narration—the film form itself.

Film and literature are, of course, two very different kinds of experiences. However, in writing *The Celluloid Literature* I have elected to concentrate on those areas that are common to both literature and the narrative film. I want this book to accomplish two goals: First, to provide the reader with an introduction to the film art and, second, to emphasize how close, both in form and in content, literature and the narrative film are to one another.

It also seems to me that the simultaneous consideration of these two closely related forms can only serve to enrich our understanding of both literature and film. The study of film can in no way diminish the important values of the more traditional literary genres; it can only serve to augment and perhaps even reinvigorate them. Film has the ability to reawaken us to the power of the sensuous image and the expressive richness of gesture and movement. In addition, it also seems clear to me that much of the methodology of literary analysis is equally applicable to the study of film. If we can simply learn to consider the film, not as an isolated phenomenon of the twentieth century, but rather as a continuation of the traditional narrative arts, we will readily discover that it has managed to retain and keep viable all that has been central to the narrative tradition.

The Celluloid Literature

Fig. I-A
The house in this shot *might* be of a sharecropper's cabin during the depression; on the other hand, it might epitomize a proud, historic survivor from our agricultural past—with only the single frame to work from, it is difficult to decide what a given picture represents. See page 9.
American Stock Photos

THE WORD AND THE IMAGE:

LANGUAGE

"In the novel, you start with a bag of words, and the way you put the words together has meaning. In the movies, you get another kind of vocabulary. You have little bits of film strips, each the equivalent of words— five words or five thousand. But the strips are put together as individual words. Constructing a movie out of the field of experience that you have recorded gets to be wholly fascinating because you are working with a brand new vocabulary. You are putting things together in a way that nobody has ever put them together before.[1]"

NORMAN MAILER

One of the exciting
features of the
film experience is its
immediacy—the
fact that the film is
occurring *right
now.* Here, a group of
Algerian nationalists
attack French
soldiers in Gillo
Pontecorvo's 1968
Battle of Algiers.

Courtesy of Audio Film Center/
Ideal Pictures

Rarely has one man been so totally part of a film as Orson Welles was in *Citizen Kane* (1941) which he produced, directed, co-wrote, and starred in. Here, Kane (portrayed by Welles) marries his first wife (played by Ruth Warrick) on the White House Lawn.

Courtesy of Janus Films, Inc.

The literal-mindedness of the camera tends to wed the character and the role forever. It is, for example, very difficult to imagine *The Graduate* without Dustin Hoffman.

No one would argue that film and literature are the same medium or even the same kinds of experience. The primary thrust of literature is linguistic, hence indirect, while the impetus of film is imagistic and immediate. And yet, despite the obvious differences which separate these two genres, there are, at the same time, some rather striking resemblances between them.

Even though the novel, as a form, has been in existence for something over a hundred and fifty years longer than the film, the two disciplines have frequently overlapped and influenced each other. David Wark Griffith, one of the truly great innovators of the film art, was once questioned about his rather unique style of editing; by way of explanation Griffith was reported to have said, "Doesn't Dickens write that way?"[2] Somewhat later, the Russian director and film theoretician, Sergei Eisenstein, in a now famous essay entitled "Dickens, Griffith and the Film Today" analyzed in detail the thematic and stylistic similarities of Griffith and Dickens. Basically what Eisenstein was pointing out was that Griffith had managed to discover cinematic equivalents for Dickens' novelistic techniques.

Eisenstein, a great innovator in his own right, acknowledged that the structure of his own highly acclaimed *Potemkin* (1926) was modelled on the five-act division of classical tragedy.[3] Eisenstein, in his observations on Griffith, as well as in his own work, recognized that the problems of artistic control presented by the film form are not unlike those inherent in the more traditional narrative arts. So it is not surprising that an increasing number of contemporary novelists and playwrights have turned their attention to the film: Jean Cocteau *(Blood of the Poet,* 1932); Alain Robbe-Grillet *(Last Year at Marienbad,* 1961); Samuel Beckett *(Film,* 1964); Norman Mailer *(Maidstone,* 1969). The novelist's attraction for the film form is readily understandable since both genres must contend with similar problems: plot, dramatization of idea, and highly individualized studies of character.

Literary classifications, such as *the novel, drama* and *poetry,* are useful, for they help to isolate what is unique to a particular form. However, classifications can, at the same time, work to obscure the numerous similarities that do exist between forms. It is important to remember that a new genre rarely springs from a vacuum; when examined closely, it usually reveals a debt to an earlier and more rudimentary form. Contemporary theater, for example, would appear to have little in common with the church, but the drama did in fact originate in religious ritual.

Greek drama, from which most of Western drama derives its character, evolved from the ceremonial worship of the god Dionysus.

Similarly, it is often forgotten that the modern novel is something less than a "pure" form even though it is over two hundred years old. The very word *novel* is borrowed: it is derived from the Italian word *novella,* a type of Renaissance prose tale such as is found in Boccaccio's *Decameron.* The novel's borrowings, in fact, were rather extensive. It made use of elements from the pastoral romance of the Hellenistic Greeks (Apuleius' *Golden Ass*); the courtly fictions of Malory and the travel romances of Sir John Mandeville; the Spanish picaresque tales such as *Don Quixote;* the sketches of "characters" by Sir Thomas Overbury and John Earle; the bourgeois fiction of Thomas Deloney; the domestic literature of roguery as exemplified by Greene and Dekker; the English essay, particularly the Sir Roger de Coverley papers from *The Spectator;* allegories such as *Pilgrim's Progress,* and the jest books and chapbooks of unprofessional literatures.[4]

Like the novel, the film evolved from mixed ancestry. Discoverable in its form are elements from drama—staging, dialogue, gesture and movement; from painting—arrangement, shape, form, texture, color and lighting; from poetry—symbolism, metaphor and other literary tropes; from music—rhythm and counterpoint, and, of course, from fiction—structure, narration, theme and characterization. The film, though, had a particularly decisive advantage over the novel: since the novel developed earlier, the film could draw upon its techniques and discoveries. Susan Sontag, in her *Against Interpretation,* has even gone so far as to argue that the history of the cinema is, in a sense, a repetition of the history of the novel.

> The fifty years of the cinema present us with a scrambled recapitulation of the more than two hundred year history of the novel. In D. W. Griffith, the cinema had its Samuel Richardson [one of the so-called fathers of the novel]; the director of *Birth of a Nation* (1915), *Intolerance* (1916), *Broken Blossoms* (1919), *Way Down East* (1920), *One Exciting Night* (1922), and hundreds of other films voiced many of the same moral conceptions and occupied an approximately similar position with respect to the development of the film art as the author of *Pamela* and *Clarissa* [Samuel Richardson] did with respect to the development of the novel.[5]

This, of course, is not to argue that every great director can be matched with a great novelist, but simply to note that the film, in a highly accelerated manner, was able to draw upon the history of narrative fiction.

Both the novel as well as the film found their most responsive audiences in the middle classes. As they were both considered "popular" forms, they were, to a great extent, ignored by scholars and serious students of the arts. As might be expected, the values, aspirations, and tragedies of middle class life were often reflected in both genres. Martin Day comments on the response of the burgeoning middle class to the novel:

> The 18th century saw a vastly increased reading public chiefly of the middle class. Practical and down-to-earth, this class wanted to read about people it could recognize from its own observations and describe in the language it employed. It preferred its stories to end with financial and domestic rewards, its own clear-cut goals in life.[6]

Pamela, or Virtue Rewarded (1740-1741) by Samuel Richardson, the novelist to whom Miss Sontag compared D. W. Griffith, tends to substantiate Day's observations. Though the novel's form is highly inventive, its substance is cloyingly sentimental. Pamela Andrews originates from a lower middle-class family, whereas Squire B——, her employer, represents the landed gentry. The novel's storyline, Squire B——'s attempts to seduce Pamela, is highly melodramatic. Pamela, however, successfully manages to defend her virtue against the machinations of her employer, and, at the end of Part One, triumphantly leads the jaded rake, now a devoted suitor, to the altar. Honor is defended, virtue triumphs, and a young girl manages to better her class position.

Other novels of the 18th century, with a broader base of subject matter, were avidly consumed by an expanding reading population. Familiar scenes of English life were depicted in such works as Goldsmith's *The Vicar of Wakefield* (1762; 1766), and Mackenzie's *The Man of Feeling* (1771). Novels of adventure, Defoe's *Robinson Crusoe* (1719) and Smollett's *Roderick Random* (1748), were highly popular. Tales of terror and the supernatural, Walpole's *Castle of Otranto* (1764) and Radcliffe's *Mysteries of Udolpho* (1794) gratified the public's penchant for the bizarre and the fanciful. Narratives set on the continent and in the Orient, Smollett's *Travels through France and Italy* (1766) and Beckford's *Vatek: An Arabian Tale* (1781-1782), transposed the English sensibility to foreign locales.

If the early novels and films were appealing to audiences of similar interests and sensibilities (despite the time differential), it might be expected that there would be similarities in subject matter. Kenneth MacGowan, in his *Behind The Screen,* lists some of the early programs that were being shown at Foster & Bial's Music Hall in the 1890's:

Sea Waves	Venice, Showing Gondolas
Umbrella Dance	Kaiser Wilhelm, reviewing his troops
The Barber Shop	Skirt Dance
Burlesque Boxing	Butterfly Dance
Monroe Doctrine	The Bar Room
A Boxing Bout	Cuba Libre[7]

As in the early novels, the familiar is recognized in the early film program: "Sea Waves," "The Barber Shop," and "A Boxing Bout," and, in addition, foreign settings are utilized: "Venice, Showing Gondolas," and "Kaiser Wilhelm, Reviewing His Troops."

That the early films and the novels could share similarities in origin, utilize similar narrative devices, and even analogous subject matter, might be expected, perhaps even predicted. What does come as a surprise, however, is the observation that the film and the novel attain meaning similarly even though they employ quite dissimilar techniques.

If the obvious is set aside momentarily—that film is essentially a visual experience whereas literature is a linguistic one—it would be very useful to examine the elements, or languages, of these two experiences. An examination of these components places the reader or the viewer in a better position to evaluate how the total experience was achieved.

In a study of the aesthetics of poetry, Ezra Pound devoted a portion of his *ABC of Reading* to a consideration of the Chinese ideogram. By examining the ideogram, Pound was able to point up economically and graphically an essential characteristic of poetry—that the ideogram "means the thing or the action or situation, or quality . . . that it pictures:"[8]

   sun tangled in the tree's branches, as at sunrise, meaning now the east

man   tree   sun

With a Chinese ideogram, the reader receives both the symbol (the ideogram itself) and the object represented (the suggestive image) simultaneously. No one would be apt to confuse the symbol (人) for a man, and yet clearly there is an attempt to represent the configuration of a man. The same consideration might be applied to the film representation of a man. Who would, for example, confuse a close-up of a man's face (represented on the screen by a twenty-five-foot tall image) for the actual man? Thus, every narrative must take the form of *mimesis*—that is, an imitation of nature—or move toward invention, the creation of an unprecedented depiction of reality—or a combination of the two. Hence, nothing can be the represented object except for the object itself (a variation of Gertrude Stein's "A Rose is a Rose, is a Rose"); consequently, all art must be either a representation of reality (mimesis) or the creation of an entirely different reality.

The word and the image are similar in that they are both visual phenomena—they must both be perceived with the eyes. On one hand, the verbal "image" *farmhouse* demands that the reader "convert" the lifeless and yet suggestible word into an approximation of what the author intended. Transposing a word to an internalized image will necessarily evoke a highly individualized response because everyone's experience of a farmhouse differs. To a boy raised in a city slum, *farmhouse* might mean "health," "contentment," "peace"; to a countryboy who left home, it might mean "chores," "boredom," "endless, mindless drudgery." In short, the word "farmhouse" will be interpreted by the reader for himself.

On the other hand, it would seem that the film maker is able to exert a greater degree of control over his medium than the writer since the image of a farmhouse is much more explicit than the word itself. That is, it is not necessary to translate a picture into an image—film is literal, concrete and explicit. The film maker is able to show precisely the farmhouse he has in mind—he doesn't have to trust that the reader will "see" the same farmhouse. And yet, despite his superior technical ability to delineate the concrete, the film maker gives up some of his power of suggestion by insisting on explicitness.

For example, a novelist might write: "The weathered red barn in back of the house somehow always gave me a comforting feeling of security whenever I looked at it." The film maker can present a barn that is visually attractive, solid in appearance, but he cannot depend on his viewer to perceive the barn as an emblem of security unless he is willing to have an off-camera voice blatantly announce: "Please view this barn as a symbol of security." Yet despite the differing degrees of explicitness and connotative control, both artists must work with languages that function, in many ways, in a remarkably similar fashion.

For the writer, the most integral unit of creation is the *word:* it is the word from which he creates his sentences, paragraphs, chapters and, ultimately, his book. For the film maker, the basic building block is the *frame*—a single transparent picture on a strip of film. Isolated, both the word and the frame have meaning, but that meaning is imprecise—it lacks a context.

The word "quiver," for example, could be a reference to either a case for holding arrows—in which instance it would be a noun—or it might describe a particular kind of action as a verb. Even if the reader is able to assume that what he is dealing with is a verb rather than a noun, the ambiguity is still unresolved, for the reader is still unclear as to the nature of the verb. The verb could be indicating the movement that an arrow describes when it comes to rest, or simply the nature of a motion like a shaking movement—a tremor. Even if the reader is further advised that the verb is not describing the motion of an arrow, he still isn't quite sure as to how to perceive the essential character of the quivering movement—the tremor. If this motion, for example, describes a leaf it is one thing; if it describes, on the other hand, a girl, it is something else again, for the tremor could be simply a reaction to the cold, or perhaps even the reaction to a fright—there even exists the possibility that it might be a combination of both fear and inclement weather.

Again, it might appear that no such problem would exist because of the explicitness of the frame—it provides far more information than the single ambiguous word. And yet notice what actually does happen when a viewer is confronted with the single frame. In Figure I-A the viewer sees the image of a cabin. The cabin appears to be unpainted pine with a wood shingled roof, and from the outside the cabin appears to be a single large room. A simple chimney runs up the side of the windowless cabin. The background appears to be bean fields. The image might represent a sharecropper's house during the early depression days, and even if it does, despite the viewer's assurance of *what* he is seeing, there still some doubt as to *how* to see the cabin. With only the single frame from which to work, it is very difficult to decide in what kind of context the picture needs to be placed because several possibilities exist.

Perhaps the viewer is supposed to perceive the house as a nostalgic memory of a less complicated, less anxiety-ridden past. In this case, the frame might be seen with the kind of hard and yet simple beauty that James Agee[9] captured so well in his *Let Us Now Praise Famous Men*.

The house may appear in a documentary concerning the conditions of poverty in the United States and, in this instance, the house is not a remnant of the past, but an eyesore in the present. It is a testimony to the discrepancies that exist between the "Haves" and the "Have-nots." Here the viewer would see the "shack" in the house, would probably feel sympathy or sorrow, perhaps even indignation.

The house may also appear in another kind of documentary—one produced by a government bureau, concerning the history of farming in the United States. Now the cabin represents only a survival of the historic past—an artifact. In this instance, the house (no longer a shack, notice) may well evoke pleasure on the part of the viewer. In comparing the contemporary farm dwellings with the cabin, the viewer is even made to feel proud that the standard of living has been raised so substantially. Just as the reader would need to see "quiver" in the context of a sentence before he could be clear about the meaning of the word, the viewer would need to see the single frame of the farmhouse within the context of the shot.

A sentence typically clarifies the meaning of an individual word, sets it in a more meaningful perspective. In a complete sentence the word "quiver" would attain a more explicit meaning: *She quivered slightly at the coolness of the night air, then proceeded alone up the deserted street.* From this sentence, it is clear that the girl's quivering is the result of the night air, that the motion is a sign of physical discomfort. And yet, at the same time, the sentence is also colored slightly by the phrase *then proceeded alone up the deserted street.* The additional information—that she is alone, that it is dark, quiet and chilly—suggests a feeling of fear, of foreboding. Thus, in the last analysis, the word "quivered" seems to convey both physical discomfort and fear.

In order to provide the same degree of clarity for the film viewer, it would be necessary for him to see *a shot*—a fragment of a film which has been taken, either actually or apparently, in one uninterrupted running of the camera. For example, if a film maker were shooting an important tennis match and wanted to indicate the tension of the contest to an audience, it is very unlikely that he would follow the exchanges of the match like a spectator. He would, more likely, avoid that approach because it would not only be repetitive, monotonous and dizzying to follow, but it would probably also be completely devoid of tension —the viewer would be so caught up in the very mechanics of watching that the tension of the match would be entirely lost. It is, in other words, the same kind of response that takes place when someone is totally engaged in some dangerous activity. While the person is engaged, there is the total consuming interest; it is only when the activity or danger has passed that he is able to experience his fear. To evoke the feeling of tension inherent in the match, the film maker would probably cut extensively during the event. (A *cut* is an instantaneous transition from one shot to another and is usually easy to spot in a film because it is invariably accompanied by a shift of camera position.) In the instance of the tennis match, the film maker might open with a long shot of the two antagonists facing each other, then cut to a medium shot of the player who was serving, then perhaps to a close-up of the tension-ridden face of the player waiting to return the ball. In this instance, the slowing down and breaking up of the action—converting it into shots—has helped to convey the tension involved in the contest.

There is no average shot. A shot can be as brief as a single frame. Robert Breer's *Fist Fight* (1964), for example, uses a different shot for almost every frame in the film. On the other hand, the length of a shot is only limited by the amount of film that a cameraman, in one continuous or apparently continuous filming can shoot. French film maker Jean-Luc Godard, in his film *Weekend* (1968), reputedly used a tracking shot of a young couple in an automobile that was three hundred meters long (nearly a thousand feet of film).[10]

For a viewer, a shot of the farmhouse in question would clearly be easier to "read" than the single frame—like the sentence, the shot would provide an enlarged context. The viewer, for example, might first see the farmhouse at a distance of fifty feet or so, then perhaps the camera begins to zoom* in towards the house and stops only when the doorway of the house nearly fills the entire screen (both the establishing shot of the house and the succeeding zoom would be considered one shot). Perhaps the camera remains focused on the doorway for a moment, and soon a woman comes to the door carrying a bucket. She wears a torn, ill-fitting cotton dress, and although her body looks young, her face appears drawn and haggard, and her shoulders seem to bend forward slightly. She remains bowed in the doorway and, for a moment, looks rather vacantly in the direction of the horizon. There is something about the way she is standing that suggests a "bone-tired" kind of weariness. This shot concludes with her standing in the doorway.

All of this information has been conveyed with a single shot whose

---

*A zoom lens is a lens whose focal length can be changed, thus altering the magnification of the image.

running time might be as short as ten seconds, yet notice how much information has been conveyed with this additional footage. First, it becomes apparent that the house and its occupant are not being romanticized—the stark, weary figure of the woman precludes that kind of an interpretation. Second, although it is not impossible, it is unlikely that the footage described above represents an excerpt from a documentary concerning this nation's farming history because of the way the shot was taken. There are, for example, clues within the shot itself that suggest what the film maker is doing. The establishing shot seems to remain with the house only long enough to suggest location, then it quickly moves to the doorway of the house, implying that it is the occupant or occupants of the house who are the real focus of attention. Also, the woman in the doorway is presented in a very special way. There is the contradiction between her youthful body and prematurely aged face; there comes the realization that she carries the water to the door because she probably has no plumbing; there is pathos in the sudden knowledge that she continues to wear what is clearly a rag because she has nothing to replace it with. These very carefully selected details shape the response of the viewer just as surely as the phrase *then proceeded alone up the deserted street* alters and implements the verb *quiver*. Though the question *what* has been answered more fully in both cases, neither the shot nor the sentence really answers the other questions that are raised in the reader's and viewer's mind. But expectations of answers have been raised. Again, to answer them involves a question of providing an enlarged context.

A paragraph, a series of closely related sentences, typically gives the reader additional relevant information about a particular "key" sentence in it. In the case of the sentence about the solitary girl, a paragraph would certainly yield additional information:

> The car seemed as though it were going through death throes the way it jerked and stalled. She looked at the gas gauge and discovered the source of her problem—it read empty. She was in a section of town where even the residents stayed behind carefully locked doors at night, and her face showed apprehension as she let the car drift to the curb. After securing the car doors, she stepped out onto the sidewalk. She quivered slightly at the coolness of the night air, then proceeded alone up the deserted street.

This paragraph, it should be noted, is set up much in the same way that a film maker might conceive a five-shot scene—an interior close-up shot of the girl being jostled about in the car; another close-up of a gas gauge reading empty, followed by a shot of her tense face; a medium shot of the car drifting towards the curb; a medium close shot of the girl locking up the car and walking up the street of the deserted neighborhood. In this instance, the paragraph has revealed how the girl came to be in the particular predicament that she is in and the paragraph also confirms the implications of fear that previously were only suggested.

A *scene* is ordinarily an action which is unified around a specific action or event and, normally, is also united by considerations of a time and place. The following three-shot scene of the sharecropper's cabin would remove most of the aforementioned ambiguity as to the type of film the audience is seeing:

```
Shot #1: Medium shot of the cabin; a slow zoom shot
         stopping when the doorway of the cabin fills the
         frame. A woman, walking from the interior, appears
         in the doorway holding a pan of water. She looks
         towards the camera.
cut to:
Shot #2: Long shot of a man, perhaps a quarter of a mile
         away, walking along a dirt road that is lined
         sparsely with pines. His feet set up small, barely
         discernible puffs of dust as he walks.
cut to:
Shot #3: The woman, as she was before, looking towards the
         camera. Abruptly she tosses the water into the
         yard and returns to the darkened interior of
         the house.
```

With this scene, the viewer's speculations are, in part, resolved. No longer is it necessary for him to guess how he should "read" the information he is witnessing. The hardship, the weariness of the peoples' lives has become readily apparent. It is also apparent, from this three-shot scene, that the film maker is able to approach the kind of artistic control that is ordinarily only associated with the novelist.

For a novelist, there are virtually no physical limitations on what he is able to describe; he can, in fact, set on paper whatever he is capable of imagining. The dramatist, however, cannot, for the form with which he works imposes certain limitations upon him. The dramatist cannot, for example, show the husband returning home—this would have to be eliminated or indicated by means of dialogue. In addition, the film maker's control of his material, like that of the novelist's, is more extensive. The dramatist would not be able to forcibly bring our attention to bear on the woman standing in the doorway as the film maker has done. The dramatist, rather, would have to "attract" his audience's attention by means of placement of actors and actresses, staging, dialogue, or perhaps by the use of lighting. The same considerations, of course, would hold true for the girl stranded in the forbidding neighborhood. Unless he were willing to go to a great deal of trouble, the dramatist would not be able to stage that particular scene. Again, he would be dependent upon dialogue to relate the information to the audience. To the film maker, however, this scene could be easily realized.

Eventually the novelist will combine his paragraphs into larger units—chapters. In many respects, the chapter resembles an expanded paragraph. It is usually unified by considerations of relatedness. A chapter could derive its unification from a single incident or event; it might cover the events of a particular period of time: an hour, day, year, or even a generation. A chapter could limit itself to only a single character. Sometimes relatedness can be achieved by means of a physical setting: a room, a town, or a country.

In the example of the stranded girl, it might be discovered that the episode of her running out of gas was just one of many similar unpleasant occurrences. Earlier in the chapter, she may have been threatened over the telephone. Sometime later, an inexplicable fire takes place in the kitchen of her house while she is asleep. While crossing the street, she narrowly averts being run over by an automobile. Finally, she runs out of gas in a dangerous neighborhood. All of these incidents might have one thing in common: the deliberate terrorizing of the girl. Thus, the incidents form a common thread that unifies the chapter into a coherent whole.

Chapters, like paragraphs, are distinct divisions of a novel and are usually characterized by coherence, unity and completeness. It is difficult, however, to say *exactly* what it is that distinguishes a paragraph from a chapter. Typically, the chapter is much longer than a paragraph, but there are instances of chapters in novels being no longer than a couple of sentences (Sterne's *Tristram Shandy* and Ken Kesey's *One Flew Over the Cuckoo's Nest* are two obvious examples). The problem is even more complicated when the *sequence*—the film's equivalent of the chapter—is considered.

The film, for example, does not have its narrative neatly divided into chapters (although British film maker, Lindsay Anderson, in a film entitled *If* . . . (1969) did utilize an eight-part chapter-like division). The sequence—a series of closely related scenes—is subject to precisely the same criteria as the chapter: namely, unity, coherence, and completeness. In some instances, such as Anderson's *If* . . ., or Stanley Kubrick's *2001: A Space Odyssey* (1969) with its three-part sequence division, the separation between sequences is apparent. In most films, however, it is more difficult to recognize and define the divisions.

The previously described scene of the sharecroppers would, most likely, represent a part of a sequence. The entire film, for example, might be composed of three thirty-minute sequences. The first sequence, which would include the previously described scene, would depict the poverty and deprivation of a single family. This first sequence might conclude with the family's decision to move North to a large city, and hopefully, a better life. The second sequence would describe their journey to the North, while the third sequence would reveal the protagonists in their new environment. Like chapters in a novel, the possibilities for creating sequences are virtually unlimited; the artist needs merely to suggest the relationship of one scene to another.

In order to compare the language of film with the language of literature, it was necessary to ignore, for the most part, the very striking dissimilarities of the two genres. Although a metaphor and a simile can enlarge perception by comparing the familiar with the unfamiliar ·or by examining something in a slightly altered perspective, it is essential to consider the peculiarities of each of the genres in order to determine how they differ from each other. Film is a multi-sensory communal experience emphasizing immediacy, whereas literature is a mono-sensory private experience that is more conducive to reflection.

A film is usually experienced in the presence of others who necessarily become part of the total gestalt of the film experience. Ideally, each member of the audience respects the presence of others and opens himself to the film. A tall hat, a noisy popcorn chewer, or a self-appointed narrator can adversely affect the impact of the film. The responses of the audience can also affect the perception of a film—an inappropriate laugh can provoke irritation; infectious laughter, on the other hand, can increase delight.

A novel, however, is typically a private experience; one in which the relationship between the author and the reader is relatively direct and immediate. The responses of others do not impinge on the novel in the same way that they do in the theater. The novel is also conducive to reflection as the reader can pause and consider an important passage or mull over a particular phrase. This alternative, of course, is denied the viewer because the film moves unceasingly towards its conclusion.

But the film and the novel are alike inasmuch as their order is typically linear. For the most part, the movement in the novel as well as the film could be described as sequential—events and scenes are ordered in direct relation to each other. Whether the order be A, B, C or C, B, A, the progression is straightforward. This tends to be true even if a film or novel opens with a conclusion (Orson Welles' *Citizen Kane* [1940] or Thornton Wilder's *The Bridge of San Luis Rey* come to mind—in both cases, they open with their protagonists' deaths); and even though the normal order has been reversed, the narrative will still tend to follow a relatively predictable, sequential path.

One of the exciting features of the film experience is its immediacy —the fact that the film is occurring *right now* before the audience's eyes. Although immediacy tends to promote greater involvement, it also has the tendency to create certain kinds of problems for the film maker. Most of the problems usually center around considerations of time.

In order to describe a peculiar habit of one of his characters, a novelist might write: "Every day for six months at precisely eleven thirty-two, he would seat himself at a park bench on 27th Avenue and count the busses that passed." The reader unquestionably accepts the suggested duration of time; in other words, to the reader, it seems credible. For a film maker, this sentence would pose a problem for he would have to portray, visually and convincingly, the passage of six months' time. Not only would this entail a number of shots of the man performing this activity, but it would also be necessary to indicate, within the shots, the passage of time. Typically, this is accomplished by use of the background: trees blooming, leaves falling, then, finally, the stark, leafless, skeletal trees of winter. The changing attire of the man— short-sleeved shirt to jacket to overcoat—would also support this impression.

Conversely, a novelist could conceivably devote an entire chapter to an event that actually took only seconds to transpire. A man nearly drowns. As he struggles to the surface and subsequently sinks again, the events of his life flit through his mind. Despite the fact that it might take an entire chapter to describe what he thought, a reader would have no problem in accepting this chapter as credible. The film maker, however, cannot take advantage of this particular convention. If he moves the scene too rapidly, then the viewer loses the density of the experience that occurred during the event. If the film maker takes too much time with the scene, the credibility of the entire scene is called into question. Robert Enrico in his Cannes Film Festival Award-winning short film, *Occurrence at Owl Creek Bridge* (1961), does manage to successfully "stretch" the passage of a second or two into seventeen minutes but, in order to accomplish this feat, it is necessary for him to deceive the viewer. The viewer believes that he is witnessing the miraculous escape of a man who was almost hanged, when, in fact, he is actually witnessing an internalized fantasy of a condemned man at the gallows.

It is a relatively easy task for the novelist to manipulate time. He can, for example, utilize a narrator who simultaneously tells a story from two vantage points. The narrator could relate events that happened to him when he was seventeen as though he were again experiencing those same events in the present. The narrator, however, is now twenty-seven and the distance from the experience is ten years. Nevertheless, the writer can alternate between these two mentalities (the seventeen-year-old and the twenty-seven-year-old—as, for instance, John Updike does in his highly praised short story, *Flight*) with little difficulty. The film maker, however, will usually select one or the other. Although it is possible to accompany the earlier scene with the voice of the older narrator, a quite different effect than the novelist's dual narrator is produced. The "voice over" tends to undermine the immediacy of the earlier scene.

Technically speaking, all film time is present time; that is, past, present, future or fantasy are all taking place now. The spectator, however, like the reader, accepts the film maker's method of representing time and, as Coleridge observed, "willingly suspends disbelief."

Not only is time employed differently in a film, but space is as well. In the novel, the reader brings his own experience to bear on the novelist's suggestions. If the novelist describes a building, the reader, having had the experience of visualizing a building, will tend to see a structure that conforms not only to the novelist's description but also to his own accumulated experience. Much of Wallace Stevens' poetry, for instance, is "about" or at least deals directly with this convention. In a film, however, the camera sees differently from either the eyes or the mind's eye, and the viewer tends to be more passive than the reader since the *conceptualization* of a scene is provided by the film.

This raises the entire question of conceptualization in the novel and the film. By its very nature, the film tends to be concrete and literal. The novel, on the other hand, is abstract and suggestive. The distinction is an important one for it means that it is very difficult for the film to deal with abstractions. A brief example might serve to point up this distinction. In one of Macbeth's most famous speeches he exclaims:

> Tomorrow and tomorrow and tomorrow
> Creeps in this petty pace from day to day,
> And all our yesterdays have lighted fools
> The way to dusty death. (Act V; sc. 5)

In the first two lines, Shakespeare has made use of personification; he describes an abstraction—tomorrow—as having the ability to creep, an activity that is usually limited to something animate. Similarly, in the following lines, he suggests that yesterdays (again, an abstraction) have "lighted fools the way to dusty death." The unusual juxtaposition of the abstract with the concrete produces a striking literary trope. A film maker obviously could have an actor deliver Macbeth's speech, but what he is unable to do is film the kind of tropes that are so common to the literary experience. How, for example, could a film maker render the following in visual terms—a sea of troubles; a dusty nothing; liberty plucking authority by the nose; a dagger of the mind? The film, of course, through metaphors, similes and symbols, does deal with abstractions, but it must necessarily render them in concrete images.

The literal-mindedness of the camera also produces other problems. Many writers (Hawthorne in *Young Goodman Brown,* Melville in *Bartleby, the Scrivener,* and Kafka in *The Trial*)[11] have successfully created characters who are representative figures of mankind. In each of these tales, there is little physical description of the central character with the result that he becomes "universalized," an Everyman. The camera, however, produces a quite opposite effect; it tends to wed the character and the role forever. It is very difficult to imagine *La Strada* (1954) without Guilietta Masina; *The Seventh Seal* (1957) without Max Von Sydow; *The Graduate* (1968) without Dustin Hoffman. Likewise, it is not enough for a character to experience a particular scene as beautiful or threatening. In order to convince the viewers, the scene must actually be filmed as beautiful or threatening.

Finally, it should always be recognized that the film is a multi-dimensional experience; it combines sight and sound with movement. A film maker who is too "literary," who relies too heavily on dialogue, will produce a film that is "talky." Likewise, a film maker who doesn't understand the languages of vision and movement ends up producing a film that is static. This frequently happens when a play is made into a film. The dramatist, because of limited available space, must confine his action to a relatively small area; movement and placement of characters and props are critically important. In a film, however, "the entire world is a stage," and the film maker who ignores this creates a film that seems to the viewer to be unnecessarily restricted and confined.

REFERENCES

1. Roddy, Joseph, "The Latest Model Mailer," *Look* (April 27, 1969), p. 25.
2. Fulton, A. R., Motion Pictures (University of Oklahoma Press, Norman, Oklahoma, 1960), p. 79.
3. Eisenstein, Sergi, *Potemkin* (Simon & Schuster, New York, 1968), p. 8.
4. Day, Martin S., *History of English Literature: 1660—1837* (Doubleday, Garden City, N.Y., 1963), pp. 215—216.
5. Sontag, Susan, *Against Interpretation* (Dell, New York, 1966), p. 242.
6. Day, p. 217.
7. Macgowan, Kenneth, *Behind the Screen* (Dell, New York, 1965), p. 87.
8. Pound, Ezra, *ABC of Reading* (New Directions, New York, 1960), p. 21.
9. James Agee was one man who was at home both with the novel and the film. His *A Death in the Family* was posthumously awarded the Pulitzer Prize in 1957. He also found time to write five screenplays, the most famous of which was John Huston's *The African Queen* (1952). In addition, he was a film critic for *Time* and *The Nation*—and many people consider him the most perceptive one who ever wrote.
10. Ross, Walter, "Splicing Together Jean-Luc Godard," *Esquire* (New York, July, 1969), p. 42.
11. Kafka's *The Trial* was brought to the screen in 1962; script and direction by Orson Welles.

A. Protagonist, Narrator and the Audience are all the same person.

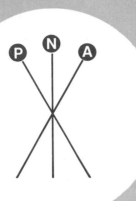

Stream of Consciousness
Interior Monologue.

FIRST PERSON

B. Protagonist, Narrator are the same person, but the Audience is now someone else.

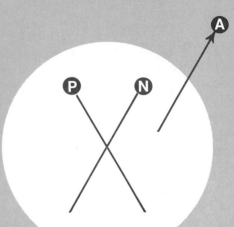

First Person,
Narrator-Protagonist.

FIRST PERSON

C. The Narrator is not the same person as the Protagonist. The Audience, as well, is someone else.

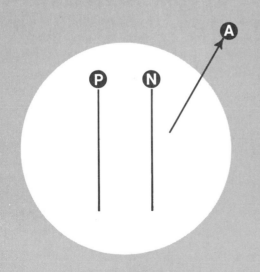

The Narrator Participant,
The Observer, The Witness.

FIRST PERSON

D. Narrator now appears to be outside the events of the story. Protagonist is observed. The Audience, again is someone else.

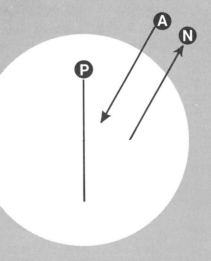

The Detached Narrator, the "Camera-Eye,"
The "Fly-on-the-Wall."

THIRD PERSON

2

POINT OF VIEW:

NARRATION AND CAMERA EYE

❝❝ When you tell the same story through the eyes of different characters, you not only have a different novel but a different reality.[1] ❞❞

NORMAN MAILER

Fig. II-E
For a 16 mm. camera,
a "normal" lens
would be 25 mm.

Fig. II-F
For a 16 mm. camera, a
wide-angle lens would
be 12.5 mm.

Fig. II-G
For a 16 mm. camera, a telephoto lens would definitely be 150 mm.

Fig. II-H
An example of the extreme wide-angle or "fish-eye" lens filmed on a 16 mm. camera.

Fig. II-K
Frontlight.

Fig. II-L
Backlight.

Fig. II-M
Sidelight.

Fig. II-N
Toplight.

Fig. II-O
Underlight.

Fig. II-P
Extreme Long Shot.

Fig. II-Q
Long Shot.

Fig. II-R
Medium Shot.

Fig. II-S
Close-up.

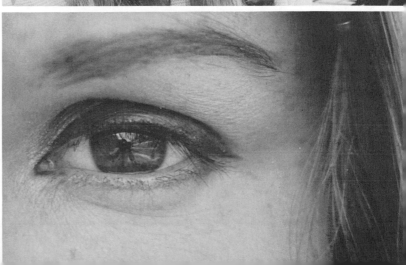

Fig. II-T
Extreme-close-up

Fig. II-I
The telephoto lens with
its ability to compress
space is frequently used
to dramatize the
density of contemporary
life.

American Stock Photos

Fig. II-J
Orson Welles' *Citizen
Kane* (1941) makes
extensive use of
symbolism. Here, Kane's
almost total
estrangement from his
second wife (played
by Dorothy Comigore) is
suggested by the
physical distance that
separates them and
by the preponderance of
"things" that have
come between them.
Gregg Toland, the
Director of Photography,
devised a lens system
that could photograph, in
sharp focus, anything
from 18 inches away from
the camera to infinity.

Courtesy of The Museum of
Modern Art/Film Stills Archive

This shot, from the beginning of Sidney Lumet's 1965 *The Pawnbroker* shows the pawnbroker (portrayed by Rod Steiger) being comforted by his sister-in-law. He has been dozing, and images of the Nazi atrocities he has survived have been flitting through his brain with a rapidity which is at first confusing to the audience.

Courtesy of Audio Film Center/ Ideal Pictures

Television has so accustomed us to news stories filmed on high-contrast, grainy footage that we associate this kind of "fast" film with events in the real world. For just this reason, Gillo Pontecorvo filmed much of his *Battle of Algiers* on "fast" stock in a documentary style.

Courtesy of Audio Film Center/ Ideal Pictures

N ITS most basic form, point of view is the vantage point from which the storyteller views his story. Clearly, the choice of point of view is a significant decision for both the novelist as well as the film maker since it essentially determines which story is going to be told. A simple example might begin to suggest some of the complexities that are involved in narrating a story.

A young girl meets her boyfriend at the house of a mutual friend, an older woman. At the meeting, the boy reveals his doubts about their relationship and suggests that they not see each other for a period of time. The girl rushes from the house and, in dashing across the street, is struck by an automobile. The boyfriend, the mutual friend, the driver of the car, the ambulance attendants, a police officer and a television reporter, all hurry to the scene of the accident. The event—the girl being struck by the automobile—is an incontestable fact; the meaning and significance of what has happened are something else entirely. There are at least four different conceptions of reality attending this event.

If the girl were to narrate the story as though she were telling it to herself, she would obviously describe the events through her own eyes. She would become an "I" that experienced joy at the coming meeting, disappointment when the boy began to express his feelings about the relationship, grief as he suggests that they should not see each other, shock as she flees the house, and, momentarily, fear—before she is struck by the car. The story, perhaps, could be told as though it were a recording of her consciousness, as though every event were channelled through her mind: "His mouth begins to work forming words that sound like 'separate for a while' and then I begin to feel a numbness around my temple and forehead—all I can think of is to run" (see Figure II-A).

The boy, on the other hand, might be describing the events to a friend, on the day after the accident. He is at a slight distance in time (one day) from what has happened and is mentally beginning to alter what actually did take place. Clearly, he is troubled by what has occurred as a result of his confession. Unlike the girl, however, who appeared to speak only to herself, the boy is speaking to a friend and the presence of the friend influences his choice of words, his manner of describing the event and his thinly disguised plea for forgiveness becomes apparent: "Of course, if I had thought for one minute that she would have run out like that, I *never* would have told her." Here, the narrator and the subject remain the same but the object of the discourse has shifted to another person—the confidant. The same pattern can be seen in the use of the diary or journal in which the writer addresses himself to a fantasized sympathetic audience (see Figure II-B).

The mutual friend's version, however, would make another story entirely. Although the friend is involved, she stands at an even greater distance from the source of primary "truth," for she knows only what she has been able to directly observe and overhear; but she is, on the other hand, more objective about what has happened than either the boy or the girl because she is not emotionally entangled in their lives. "I had known Karen from the time she was barely able to walk and Tom since he was five. . . ." Although the speaker is still an "I", a personality who experiences and feels, it is clear that the central subject of the event and the narrator are not one in the same—whereas, in the two previous examples, both narrator and subject were identical. The mutual friend is relegated to the role of the witness or observer of the event (see Figure II-C.)

That evening on the local news, a commentator shows his audience a film clip of the accident. Curious onlookers appear gathered around the periphery of the site where the girl was struck down; the camera dutifully records the girl on a stretcher being lifted into the ambulance, the distressed driver of the automobile that struck her, and the distraught boyfriend. Accompanying the film is a voice saying: "Earlier this afternoon at the corner of Elm and 27th Avenue, a young girl, Miss Karen Turnbull of 242 West 8th Street, was struck by a passing automobile." Now the voice has become nearly colorless, depersonalized, recording only the statistical information—the who, what, when, and how of the accident. The meaning of the event for the television viewer would probably be the question of who was at fault. The commentator, it should be noted, makes no attempt to place the blame. The camera, like the voice, simply records what has happened (see Figure II-D).

Unquestionably, there are other points of view from which this same story might be told. The driver of the car who has been suddenly catapulted into the lives of the couple is an obvious possibility. The story might have been told objectively (like the television camera example) with the addition of the girl's thoughts, or the boy's, or both their thoughts, or even with the addition of the thoughts of the mutual friend.

The variations on how the story might be told are not infinite, but certainly it is clear that its narrative possibilities are abundant. Every time the point of view shifts, another, quite different story is being told.

Sometimes it will be found that the meaning or even the "truth" of a story will vary according to how it is narrated. A case in point is Akira Kurosawa's *Rashomon* (1950); Kurosawa capitalizes on the subjectivity of a narrator by having the events of *Rashomon* related by four different people. Each time the story, which concerns a "rape" and violent death, is recounted, its meaning changes because each one of the narrators assumes responsibility for what has taken place. Kurosawa wisely never provides his audience with a "correct" interpretation. Rather, his film leaves the viewer with the suggestion that the "truth" or even the "reality" of an event is ultimately dependent upon who experiences that event.

Although there are many notable exceptions, the short story and the novel usually adhere to a single point of view throughout, as a shift in point of view is apt to confuse or disorient the reader. In the film, on the other hand, point of view is likely to be handled in just the opposite fashion—by the deployment of shifting points of view.

In the film, point of view must always be synonymous with camera eye, for the viewer has no choice except to witness what the camera perceives. Although point of view in film is considerably more limited than point of view in literature, film is capable of describing varying degrees of reality with memorable success.*

In its infancy, the camera was seen as a recording device incapable of anything but a mere registering of the action that took place in its field of vision. Consequently, the camera eye became much like a stiff-necked member of a theater audience who was seated third row center. Actors had entrances and exits, the action was blocked out in advance and staged, and the entire performance was viewed from an undeviating eye-level angle.

Then, during the 1920's, a number of film makers, notably F. W. Murnau, E. A. Dupont, and G. W. Pabst, began to extend the vocabulary and techniques of the narrative film. The discovery that the

---

*To most people in their twenties and almost everyone in their thirties and forties, the classical world will always "look like" a Cecil B. DeMille spectacular, be it the Athens of Pericles or the Rome of Caligula.

camera can move—right and left (a pan); up and down (a tilt); inward (a close-up); away (a long shot)—initiated an artistic revolution in film making. The rigid narrator of film, up until that point, had been anchored to a fixed position. Freeing the camera from its fixed position literally liberated the film's narrator.

Up until the liberation of the camera, everything that was filmed corresponded roughly to the objective, detached narrator of Figure II-D. Freeing the camera caused the frame (perimeter of the screen) to begin expanding and contracting as the camera moved closer to or further away from the subject. The camera could now begin to exert the kind of emotional control over its material and its spectators' attention that had usually been associated with only the novelist and the short-story writer.

To suggest the contrast between the superficial, external calm of a court witness and his internal turmoil, the camera need only move from a medium shot of the witness sitting in his chair to a close-up of his hands perspiring and nervously twisting a handkerchief. Similarly, a man might be lost in the barren terrain of the South Dakotas and the impact of his being lost goes unfelt—until the camera moves from a medium shot of the man to a long shot of the bleakness and desolation of the territory surrounding the man. It is at this point that the viewer really begins to experience the hopeless loneliness of his predicament.

Not long after the camera began to be used in this fashion, film makers began to discover that the camera does not have to be a passive witness to the world, but can assume an active role in the depiction of reality. The camera began adopting vantage points that literally corresponded with the narrator's point of view. Film makers found, for example, that they were able to simulate a child's view of the world simply by altering the height of the camera—if it were lowered and angled upward, adults and objects could be made to appear enormous.

Although the placing of the camera can powerfully suggest, as well as comment upon, a character or scene, it still restricts the camera to observable reality. Another significant breakthrough in the film experience occurred when film makers began to examine subjective states of reality, dreams, memories, fantasies and altered states of consciousness. As they began to investigate and explore various levels of subjective reality, they began to be able to reflect the mind's alteration between fantasy and reality. Many of these early attempts to convey subjective states of mind, however, were blatantly staged: A character might stand meditatively before the camera; the audience would witness his image beginning to ripple, and then observe the same character, now much younger, at some point in his past. This technique is, of course, the flashback—an attempt to indicate the effect of the past on the present. Contemporary film makers no longer feel the necessity to "introduce" flashbacks, memories and fantasies; they simply let them occur.

In Sidney Lumet's *The Pawnbroker* (1965), for example, there are at first many instances of extremely rapid cuts that reveal the agonized recollections of an elderly Jew who had spent a period of time in a concentration camp. Initially, the viewer is totally unprepared for these memories. The pawnbroker (played by Rod Steiger) is sitting comfortably in a lawn chair in the backyard of a suburban home and suddenly memories of the concentration camp experience flit through his mind. The cuts are so quick (probably as short as five or six frames) that the viewer is not even quite sure of what he has seen. It is only through an accumulation of these shots that the viewer begins to piece together the gruesome reality of the pawnbroker's past.

Robert Enrico, director of *Occurrence at Owl Creek Bridge,* devotes the greater proportion of his film to a fantasized escape by the film's protagonist. Unlike Lumet, Enrico does indicate to the audience that a distortion of reality is being introduced: The sound track is slowed down, the Union soldiers on the bridge move in slow motion. But it is only at the conclusion of the film, when the viewer finally realizes that what he has seen are the escape fantasies of a by-now dead man, that he becomes really aware of the significance of the distortions that have been introduced.

An English film, *Billy Liar* (1963), alternates between the fantasies and the reality of the life of a young clerk in the undertaker's business. At one particularly frustrating point in the film, Billy imagines himself dressed in a trooper's uniform machine gunning his tormentors. More recently, Roger Corman's *The Trip* (1967) and Dennis Hopper's *Easy Rider* (1969), have attempted to portray the altered mental states produced by "mind expanding drugs". Numerous "psychedelic" effects are introduced by way of rapid cutting, distortional lenses and the use of various kinds of film stocks.

Each of the techniques described above—the memory, the dream, the fantasy and the drug experience—are the film's equivalent for the stream of consciousness technique described in Figure II-A. Each is an attempt to reveal the inner workings of an individual's mind, and each suggests the complex interplay between illusion and reality.

The camera as an "I" narrator is not witnessed too frequently, but it has been done, most notably in Robert Montgomery's 1946 adaptation of Raymond Chandler's *The Lady in the Lake*. In this instance, the viewer "becomes" the protagonist; what the camera is "seeing" the protagonist is seeing, and since the viewer is seeing through the "eyes" of the protagonist, he, in a sense, becomes the protagonist. Arthur Knight, in his *The Liveliest Art*, discusses an early application of the first-person technique in Reuben Mamoulian's *Dr. Jekyll and Mr. Hyde* (1932):

> . . . the entire first reel was shot in the first-person technique, the camera assuming the identity of Dr. Jekyll. From that position we see his hands as he plays the organ, the shadow of his head upon the music rack. When Jekyll is ready to go out, the butler hands hat, cloak and cane directly to the camera.[2]

The use of the camera as the subjective narrator seems to be most effective when it is used sparingly. Unlike the short story and novel, which can simultaneously maintain both the narrator-as-storyteller and the narrator-as-main-participant, the film must, in a sense, efface both the narrator as a reflecting personality and, to a large extent, the character as participant in the action (as in the *Dr. Jekyll and Mr. Hyde* example), in order to use the narrative technique described in Figure II-B.

Although film can employ the narrational technique of the witness or narrator-participant (Figure II-C), many of the same problems that plague the first-person narrator hamper the narrator-participant. It would be easy enough to imagine a group of men gathered about a table in a tavern listening to the narrator. Again, the camera could be placed in such a manner to convey the impression that it is the narrator. The men at the table look attentively at the camera; occasionally clouds of smoke obscure the camera as the narrator lights his pipe. The audience hears the voice of the narrator: "I want to tell you about a remarkable young man that I met in South Africa last year." At this point the narrator-participant is fulfilling the same function as his fictional equivalent: he is a personality, shaping the responses of the listener ("a remarkable young man"), indicating to his audience that the story is the young man's and not his own ("I want to tell you about . . ."), and it is clear that he is telling the story. However, when the story shifts to the past, as it must, the narrator-participant must either be in or out of the story. If he is in, then the audience loses the editorializing of the narrator: "I thought it was strange when he told me that he would be leaving for Zanzibar the following Thursday, but I wasn't to realize until much later, the real significance of his sudden departure." Here, it is apparent that there are two mentalities operating within the same narrator: (1) what the narrator-as-fallible-human thought at the time the event occurred and, (2) what he now knows as a result of further experience or information. The film maker can, of course, return the audience to the table in the tavern but, obviously, he must interrupt the action to do so. If the narrator-participant is out of the action, then there are the same limitations that restricted the first-person narrator mentioned above.

An objective or detached narrator (Figure II-D) is most frequently used by the film maker. This technique most clearly maximizes the camera's narrative potentialities while minimizing its limitations. The camera can view things microscopically, as in the case of an extreme close-up, or it can shift to a vast overview of its subject with a panoramic shot or even an aerial view. Thus, it is able to achieve a kind of omnipotence that is frequently associated with the objective or detached narrator. There is usually no editorializing, except for selectivity, and the audience is simply shown the events of the story. Utilizing this point of view allows the camera its greatest latitude of freedom, for exclusive use of any one point of view in film will necessarily impose certain limitations. For example, if the camera is being used to record the point of view of the protagonist, then the camera is obviously restricted only to what that individual would be capable of perceiving. To use an aerial shot would necessitate putting the protagonist in an airplane; to have the protagonist see himself would only be possible if he looked in a mirror, saw a picture of himself or imagined himself in a dream or a flashback. With the detached or objective narrator (a technique that is sometimes called the "camera eye"), the camera can conceivably adopt any point of view—take on the omnipotence of a god-like narrator, become capable of viewing the action regardless of time or geographical limitations. It can, for example, show a character in the living room of his home and suddenly shift to an aerial shot of the community in which the character lives. Likewise, if the character is thinking about his brother who is traveling through Europe, the camera can literally show the audience the brother riding on a train through Southern France.

Most of the films that an audience views today combine a variety of points of view, but the spine of the narrational technique is usually the detached, objective narrator. However, a film that employs only the detached narrational technique lacks intimacy; working at a distance, it curtails the viewer's involvement. And a film that restricts itself to a first-person subjective narration imposes unnecessary limitations on the story—the experience is much like trying to view the world through the eyepiece of a telescope, undoubtedly interesting, but constricting.

It cannot be emphasized too strongly that point of view is of critical importance to the artist because it determines not only which story is to be told but, to a great extent, how it will be told. Point of view resembles, in some ways, the parable of the six blind men who attempt to describe the elephant: the man who seizes upon the trunk remarks that the elephant is very much like a snake, the man who feels the elephant's side disagrees because, to him, the elephant is more like a wall, and another, who is touching the elephant's leg, argues that both of his companions are in error for the elephant is most assuredly like a tree trunk. Clearly, where each of the men was positioned in relation to the elephant determines the "story" he will narrate.

Once the film maker has determined which story he wishes to tell, he must then direct his attention to a consideration of how that story must be told. Since his story is to be related in a visual language, he must consider what images best convey it.[3] Manipulation of visual images involves predominantly the consideration of six factors: (1) the choice of camera lens; (2) the kind, intensity, and direction of light selected; (3) the type of film stock to be employed; (4) the angle of the camera in relation to the subject; (5) the distance of the subject from the camera, and (6) the speed at which the camera is being run when the subject is filmed.

The "heart" of any camera is its lens, for it is the lens which determines the kind of image that will be transferred from the outside world onto the film. The lens is frequently referred to as the "eye" of the camera. This can be a useful analogy, for the lens in many ways does emulate the functions of the human eye. On the other hand, the analogy is somewhat misleading because the camera lens records the world in a slightly different fashion than the eye. The human eye is a much more versatile lens than the lens of the camera; it permits a person to change his focus instantly from an object only a few inches away to another object as far away as the horizon. Also, the eye takes in a larger area of information than most camera lenses because an individual is always viewing a field of vision of roughly 180 degrees, even though a large percentage of the scene is typically composed of two dimly perceived peripheries. The individual is usually directing his attention to a relatively small area of the 180 degree span. For example, if the individual is scanning a crowd for a friend, he is only faintly aware of the vast panorama of people present because his area of concentration is usually limited to the space of five or six people at a time; were he simply to take stock of the crowd, he would be seeing very differently.

A film maker has at his disposal many different kinds of lenses, each of which will significantly alter the way in which a given shot will be perceived. The choice of lens will usually be determined by two basic considerations: (1) the magnitude of the image desired—its size, and (2) the effect of the lens on perspective—the ways in which it will alter "normal" perspective.

Consider an example of a 16 millimeter camera (most of the classroom projectors are 16 mm), and the changes that take place when different lenses are placed on the camera. For a 16 mm camera, a "normal" lens would be a 25 mm. Normal, as indicated by the quotation marks, is a relative term. A 16 mm camera equipped with a normal lens will record objects pretty much as the viewer would ordinarily perceive them if he did not attempt to narrow or enlarge the field of vision. In any given shot, the sizes of the objects would appear in ordinary perspective; objects close to the camera would, as expected, appear larger than objects further away.

Imagine a 16 mm camera set up on a lawn. About fifty feet in front of the camera, there is a girl sitting; behind, and to the right of the girl is a building. Shooting this scene with the 25 mm lens would reveal all of the girl in the center of the frame; behind the girl and to the right, the viewer would behold, in normal perspective, the building; the grassy area in front of and behind the girl would also appear in a normal perspective. Everything in the scene would be in relatively sharp focus (i.e., there would be little fuzziness or blurring perceived in the image).

Without moving the camera from its position, the film maker

changes the lens of the camera. He replaces the "normal" lens with a 12.5 mm lens—a "wide angle." Even though nothing but the lens has been altered, the change in the recorded image is rather striking. The distance from the foreground to the background appears to have been elongated; the grassy area in front of the girl seems wider than it was before and now it also looks as though the building in back of the girl is further away than in the previous shot. The viewer also notices that the sizes of the images are not as large as they were in the previous shot. Once again, all of the recorded images seem to be in sharp focus.

If the film maker again changes the lens, replacing the wide angle with a 150 mm long lens—the "telephoto"—the visuals are significantly altered. The telephoto lens functions much in the same way as a telescope does—it magnifies the image. The viewer now sees only the girl and she appears so close that the viewer could reach out and touch her. Besides the magnification of the image, the viewer notices that some other changes have taken place in the composition. The building behind the girl is not only blurry, but appears to have moved closer to the girl. The grassy area between them doesn't seem to be as wide as it was before; the grass also looks as though it were a hazy carpet of green—it is not possible to make out any individual features in the grass. To the viewer, the girl is easily the most dominant focal point in this shot—the grass and building surrounding the girl seem very subdued in comparison.

If the film maker were interested in producing an exaggerated distortional effect in this scene, he might use still another lens—the extreme wide-angle lens, or as it is sometimes called, the "fish-eye." Using the fish-eye lens, the scene, to the viewer, would now appear to resemble a world globe; the corners of the frame would be rounded; the area of information (what the viewer sees in the frame) would be increased. The shot would reveal all of the girl, the building behind the girl including part of the sky. The image itself, however, would look like nothing the viewer had ever seen before. The entire image would look spherical—the edges of the frame would appear to have been rounded off. The images in the center of the frame would seem to curve backward at the edges and bulge inward at the center. The girl for example, would look bowed.

Each of the four times that the lenses are changed, the viewer is forced to view the scene differently (see Figures II E-H). His response to the image is obviously shaped according to the way in which it has been presented to him. Which lens the film maker will select is prede-termined by what he wants to do with the scene.

If the scene is a dream or a fantasy, the film maker might choose to shoot it with the fish-eye or the telephoto lens. The distortion introduced by the fish-eye lens would lend an air of unreality to the scene that would be appropriate to a dream or fantasy. But the extreme distortion of the lens would also introduce a visual grotesqueness. If the lawn were the place of a traumatic incident, this grotesqueness might well be appro-priate. On the other hand, if the lawn represents a pleasant memory, the film maker would probably want to avoid this effect. The telephoto lens with its critical depth of field would impart a selectivity as well as an atmosphere to the scene. The atmosphere would be rather "romantic," for the less dominant aspects of the scene would be blended into a kind of impressionistic blur of color. The girl, on the other hand, would stand out in sharp relief to the blurred background. In other words, the eye of the viewer would immediately gravitate to the girl.

With the telephoto lens, the girl is selected from the overall context of the scene. This might easily be an appropriate shot if the girl has a definite relationship to the protagonist. But if the film maker wishes the girl to be only a part of the total context—the scene—he might decide to employ the wide-angle lens. The wider lens would render a stronger feeling of place because it would take in more total area.

Lens selection can also be used to impart additional meaning to a given shot. The telephoto lens with its ability to compress space has frequently been used with great success to indicate the density of con-temporary life. Shooting a crowded sidewalk or street with this lens produces a dramatic effect—the people or the automobiles appear to be virtually on top of each other (see Figure II-I). As might be expected, this lens will also affect movement.

If a camera with a telephoto lens is placed at an angle so as to view a man running, it will appear as though the runner is making very little headway. Were the man in question attempting to outrun some pursuers, this kind of shot would be not only dramatically effective, but very appropriate. The audience will probably identify with the runner. To the runner, it seems as though no matter how hard he might run, he cannot put enough distance between himself and his pursuers—and the lens, appropriately, would tend to support this impression.

The telephoto lens has also been employed dramatically to rivet the audience's attention within a shot. Imagine a camera set up in the living room of an apartment. The camera is established slightly behind and above a couch. The foreground—the area where the couch is located— is not in focus, hence blurred. In the background, in sharp focus, the audience views the wall of the apartment that faces the hallway. After a while, the audience hears a key turning in the lock, then watches the door open into the apartment. A woman enters. At this moment, the entire scene comes into sharp focus, revealing a man hidden behind the couch. A scene that had previously seemed quite mundane now takes on an aura of tension and expectation. In this example, the foreground was used to comment on the background. A film maker can easily reverse this technique and use the background to comment on the foreground.

A married woman is clandestinely meeting her lover in a small cafe. The critical focus of the camera is on the couple, who are earnestly engaged in conversation at their table. The background—the rest of the cafe—is out-of-focus. The audience watches the couple for a minute, then the camera changes focus, the foreground becomes blurred and the background comes into focus, revealing the husband of the woman seated at a table in the rear of the restaurant. The relaxed atmosphere of the cafe, for the audience, suddenly becomes charged.

As might be expected, the wide-angle lens would tend to reverse the visual effects of the telephoto or long lens. The most frequent use of the wide-angle involves outdoor shots, for the lens has the capability of taking in wider areas of information—it is clearly better suited for sweeping panoramic scenes. But, like the telephoto lens, it can also be employed to convey additional information to an interior shot.

In regard to movement, a wide-angle lens will render the impression that more of it is taking place than is, in fact, actually occurring. This distortion of movement could be very effective in certain instances. In the previously mentioned example of the runner and the pursuers, the film maker might wish to emphasize the rapid, relentless pursuit of the men who are chasing the runner rather than his slowness. By filming the pursuers with the wide-angle lens, he could make it appear as though the pursuers were moving at a tremendous rate of speed; this, of course, would also have the effect of emphasizing the plight of the runner.

Whereas the telephoto lens will make things appear to be closer together than they actually are, the wide-angle lens will convey the impression that they are farther apart. The wide-angle lens has the effect of "stretching out" an image. Again, the lens can influence the way in which a viewer will perceive a shot. If this lens is used in a large room occupied by only a few people, it would make the people appear to be farther apart from each other than they actually are. Were the film maker attempting to indicate the isolation and loneliness of these people, judicious use of the wide-angle lens would definitely tend to convey them visually (see Figure II-J).

By now it should be clear that the way in which a visual image is recorded has a great deal to do with meaning in a film. The visual effect that a particular lens produces in an image can easily be as important as what occurs or what is said in a given scene. In some instances, what the camera reveals to the audience might even be more important than what the characters are saying to each other. For example, were the film maker to use the wide-angle lens in a large drawing room with only two people present, a husband and his wife, the audience would see the couple as being far apart physically. If the husband tells the wife, "I feel close to you," the audience would tend not to believe his words, for there is clearly a discrepancy between what he is saying and what the audience is witnessing. The choice of lenses in a given shot is nearly always related to meaning.

The manner in which a shot is lighted is also related to meaning. People have always been influenced by light. A dark, gloomy day is frequently felt as being "depressing," whereas a bright, sunny day is experienced as being "uplifting." And since the inception of poetry, poets have always made use of light to render a mood or an atmosphere that is appropriate to their subjects. Daybreak is frequently related to new life; late afternoon to the waning years; night to death.* The film maker makes use of light in much the same way as the poet does.

Basically, there are two different types of lighting—natural and artificial. Natural lighting, of course, is provided by the sun, artificial lighting by electricity. Each of these two types of lighting may be used by itself or in combination. Again, the choice of lighting is determined by considerations of how the film maker wishes the scene to be perceived.

---

*Dylan Thomas' great poem to his dying father, *Do Not Go Gentle into that Good Night*, presents a striking modern example of the metaphorical use of night-as-death.

Natural lighting, for example, is not a static quantity; it is constantly changing. At sunrise and at sunset, there is usually a predominance of red tones, thus imparting a feeling of warmth to the image. At noon, on the other hand, the light tends to become flat and colorless, creating a quite different kind of visual effect. Not only does the color of the light change during the day, but also its intensity—a late afternoon sun will cast long shadows and darken certain areas of the image.

Intensity of light is most frequently used to impart a mood or an atmosphere to a scene. "Light" comedies are usually photographed in what is called "high key" lighting, that is, lighting that is bright and unshadowed. The brightness of the lighting is appropriate to the lightness of the subject.

On the other hand, most "horror" movies will employ "low key" lighting in order to create dark, heavily shadowed visuals. This kind of lighting usually produces a feeling of mystery and foreboding. Obviously, the use of high and low key lighting is not restricted to comedies and horror films. The melancholy films of Ingmar Bergman, predictably, make extensive use of "low key" lighting, but both Federico Fellini (*La Dolce Vita* [1959]) and Alain Resnais (*Last Year at Marienbad* [1961]) have successfully employed "high key" lighting in films that are serious and somber.

As might be expected, white light is not a homogenous substance, but rather a mixture of seven colors: red, orange, yellow, green, blue, indigo, and violet. The reds are the strongest rays in the spectrum, whereas the violets are the weakest. By using a filter, a film maker can, to a great extent, control and alter the visual impact of a given shot (this holds true for black-and-white films as well as color). A filter, typically a piece of dyed glass that is placed in front of the camera's lens, performs a negative function, that is, it removes certain rays in the color spectrum. Effective employment of a filter can make a significant contribution to a visual composition.

For example, if a film maker were to use a red filter in an outdoor shot, the filter would considerably darken the sky producing an ominous and threatening sky. On the other hand, a green filter would have a tendency to increase color contrast and yet soften the light contrasts. Richard Lester, a British film maker, made suggestive use of a filter in *Petulia* (1967). One scene shows a couple shopping in an all-night grocery store in San Francisco. The store is one of those emporiums that are crammed with a plethora of canned goods, instant foods, and cellophaned vegetables. Its interior is dominated by whites; walls and ceiling, display cases, uniforms, goods and check-out stands all indicate an otherworldly whiteness. Lester employs a filter that causes the shot to be dominated by blue tones. The result is eerie: A relatively ordinary grocery store suddenly becomes viewed as an alien, cold, almost frighteningly dehumanized landscape—an exact counterpart, in fact, of the spiritual wastelands Petulia, her husband, and her lover inhabit. Thus, the use of filters as a means of controlling light values can assuredly alter how a shot will be understood by a viewer.

Light, of course, always emanates from a source, be it the sun or a floodlight. Again, how that light strikes a subject is critically important for, like the lenses and the filters, it will determine how a viewer will perceive any given image.

Basically, there are five ways by which a subject can be illuminated: frontlight, backlight, toplight, sidelight, and underlight. Each of these methods has to do with the relationship (angle) of the source of light with the subject. An easy and instructive experiment would be to make your own study of the effect of lighting on a subject. In a semi-darkened room (a bathroom would serve nicely), stand before a mirror with a desk lamp or flashlight. Hold the light directly in front of your face (frontlight—Figure II-K) and study the effects of the light on your face. Notice that your face appears to be normally lighted, that the image in the mirror is, in the main, unshadowed and complimentary. Any shadows cast by the light fall behind your face and are, for the most part, unnoticed.

Now move the light directly in back of your head (backlight—Figure II-L). You will notice that there is a rim of light around your hair and the sides of your face—visually the effect is much like a halo. But notice also that your face is now evenly shadowed as the light source is coming from behind. If the light source is then moved to the side (sidelight—Figure II-M), another quite different effect is created. Your face is now evenly split into half light and half dark.

Moving the illumination directly over your head (toplight—Figure II-N), again alters the image in the mirror. This time the hair is brightly illuminated, but only a portion of the face is lit. The prominent features —the bridge of the nose, perhaps the cheek bones as well—receive some of the spill-over light, but the remainder of the face is deeply shadowed.

Finally, move the light beneath your chin and angle it upward (underlight—Figure II-O). You will recognize this style of lighting almost immediately. The shadows are cast unnaturally upward making the face appear grotesque; the upper part of the nose, as well as the eye sockets are deeply shadowed, and the top of the head is very dark. This kind of lighting is frequently seen in horror movies.

Varying the light in this manner not only significantly alters the visual impact of a shot, but it also helps to reveal character. Ralph Stephenson and J. R. Debrix in *The Cinema As Art* comment upon the effect of light on the human face:

> Lighting from above spiritualizes a subject and gives it a solemn or an-gelic look . . . or an air of youth and freshness. Lighting from below imparts a feeling of unease and gives a wicked or unearthly appearance. Lighting from the side gives relief and solidity to a face, but may make it ugly and show the lines. It may indicate an ambiguous personality, half good, half bad, symbolically half light, half shade. Lighting from in front blurs any faults, flattens relief, softens modelling, makes the face more beautiful, but takes away its character. Coming from behind, lighting idealizes a subject, giving it an ethereal quality. This sort of lighting is a modern version of the halo of the saints or the aura of a medium.[4]

The film stock on which the image is to be captured needs to be carefully considered by a film maker as well. Images are recorded on long strips of a plastic-like base material called celluloid or cellulose acetate. On top of the celluloid is an emulsion that contains particles which record the image.

As has been indicated, film itself comes in a variety of widths: 8 mm, 16 mm, 35 mm, 70 mm and larger. Most home movies are shot on 8 mm or super 8 film stock; classroom projectors typically use 16 mm film; the larger sizes are usually restricted to commercial productions. In general, the larger the film width, the better quality the projected image.

In addition to the size of the film, the film maker must also take into consideration the film's sensitivity to light, for this will usually determine the quality of his image. A so-called "fast" film requires less light to record an image, whereas a "slow" film requires more. However, when a "fast" film is used, it typically reveals a certain amount of graininess in the projected image. A newspaper photograph usually displays graininess—the image appears "rough" and lacks in subtle color differentiation. The "slow" film, on the other hand, produces a much more even, polished image.

Choice of film stock is intimately related to the intentions of the film maker. If a film maker were attempting to film a re-make* of James Thurber's short story *The Secret Life of Walter Mitty,* he would certainly be faced with the problem of visually indicating Mitty's sudden leaps from reality to fantasy. In Thurber's story, almost any kind of sensory suggestion—the monotonous movement of the windshield wipers, a car backfiring—is sufficient motivation to trigger one of Mitty's fantasies. One method of resolving this problem would be to use two different kinds of film—the "slow" as well as the "fast" film stock. The slower stock would record reality "naturally"—the range from black to white would be filled with all the subtle intermediate shades of grey. The faster film, on the other hand, would visually underwrite the unreality of Mitty's fantasies because many of the in-between grey tones would be lost. The choice of film stock would thus be related to content.

Because a faster film requires less light, it is frequently selected by documentarists and television cameramen (a large percentage of the six o'clock news is filmed material). Both the newsmen and the documentarists must rely heavily on natural available light as they must be free to move with the action unencumbered by bulky lighting equipment. Audiences have grown so used to witnessing documentaries and news stories on high-contrast, grainy footage that they associate this kind of film stock with "realistic" photography. Obviously, a film maker who is dealing "realistically" with a subject will keep this association in mind. John Cassavettes' *Faces* (1968), which brutally depicts the frustration and despair of a middle-class couple, makes extensive use of "fast" film stock. The result is a film that seems spontaneous and unrehearsed.

Prior to the 1960's, color stock was restricted, for the most part, to certain kinds of productions, typically musicals, sweeping historical pageants and "slick" comedies. The so-called serious films were, almost without exception, photographed in black and white. There were several reasons for this: first, color stock was more expensive, and producers displayed a marked reluctance to invest additional money in color

*Norman McLeod directed Danny Kaye in the 1947 original.

without being relatively sure that the production was going to be a popular (i.e., financial) success. Many of the productions of the serious film makers were not only frankly experimental in nature, but they were apt to deal with subjects that a general audience would find "uninteresting" or even "distasteful," with the consequence that many of the early films of today's great film makers, when first shown, were viewed by relatively small audiences.

But money was not the only reason that film makers avoided color. Color stock was much more difficult to control than black and white. Use of color not only required high-intensity lighting, but it also precluded subtle gradations of color, hence artistic control over visuals was radically diminished. There was also an unspoken sumptuary law among film makers that black and white was a more appropriate vehicle for the "serious" film. The sobriety of black and white, it was felt, contributed to the serious atmosphere of the film. Color, on the other hand, was deemed flashy and garish.

Today, most of this has changed. The cost differential between black and white and color is not as great as it was before. Technical advances have made color much more susceptible to control. And finally, an ever increasing number of film makers such as Fellini (*Juliet of the Spirits* [1964]; *Satyricon* [1970]); Antonioni (*Red Desert* [1964]; *Blow-up* [1967]; *Zabriskie Point* [1970]); Widerberg (*Elvira Madigan* [1967]) and Pasolini (*Teorema* [1968]), have produced "serious" films in color.

Today, a virtual revolution has been taking place in the film industry in regards to the use of color. It is not uncommon to see black and white used in a film that is predominantly in color. Frequently, black and white stock will be printed on color stock creating unusual tones and textures. Experimentalists, such as Stan Vanderbeek, have discovered that video tape can be subjected to a series of color wash processes and then transferred to film—and the result is an entire new range of color combinations and image qualities. Still, creative use of color in film is a relatively unexplored area.

Earlier in this chapter, it was suggested that the angle at which a camera is placed will significantly influence an audience's perception of an image. Basically, camera angle refers to the relationship between the subject and the camera. Most camera angles take their departure from a norm of an eye-level view. That is to say, if the camera is placed below eye level and angled upward, this would be designated as a *low-angle*, whereas anything above eye level, angled downward, would be described as a *high-angle*. There are, of course, gradations: A camera placed on the ground and angled upward would represent an *extreme-low-angle*, a shot from a high rooftop of the street below would be considered an *extreme-high-angle*. Although there are other possibilities, camera angle is usually related to considerations of dominance.

Consistently photographing a military commander (as Stanley Kubrick did "Colonel Jack D. Ripper"—Sterling Hayden—in *Dr. Strangelove* [1964]) from low camera angles would tend to make him appear "larger than life"; it would emphasize his stature (and his despotism). Reversal of camera angle would, predictably, produce the opposite effect. A character who is repeatedly photographed from above appears weak and inconsequential.

Camera angle has also been used to emphasize an effect or a condition. Showing the struggle of a wounded man crawling up a hill is dramatic, but angling the camera so as to emphasize the steepness of the hill more emphatically dramatizes the arduousness of his task. Similarly, if a runaway wagon containing a helpless child is plunging down a hillside, exaggeration of camera angle can contribute to the peril evoked.

Distance from camera to subject also exerts a great deal of influence on the way an audience will experience an image. Fundamentally, distances from subject to camera are divided into three broad areas: the close-up, the medium shot, and the long shot. The *long shot*, for example, might show a girl, full length, by a building. A *medium shot* would show the girl from the waist up—this shot, of course, would bring the viewer much closer to the subject. A *close-up*, more intimate yet, might show only the girl's face. Like camera angle, there are gradations that exist within these broad areas. An *extreme-long-shot* might take in much more of the area surrounding the girl; it could, for example, indicate that the girl is in front of an office. The extreme long shot contributes a stronger sense of place. A *medium-close-up* tends to be a compromise between a medium shot and a close-up. In this instance, it might show the girl from the chest to the top of her head. Finally, an *extreme-close-up* is a further division of the close-up. The entire screen would be filled with only the eye of the girl (see Figures II P-T).

Whether a given shot is considered a long shot or a close-up is a relative matter. If the subject is the Empire State Building, then a long shot might take in the entire building, whereas an extreme close-up could be an item as large as a single window.

The selection of any one shot usually touches upon the meaning of a film. In some instances, the film maker has little choice in shot selection, for the shot may be dictated by the action of a scene. If a film maker wishes to show a popular insurrection, he must necessarily film long shots of the crowd, or otherwise the impact of the numbers of people participating goes unfelt. Likewise, if a character, in a moment of excitement, reveals some startling information about himself to another character, the audience naturally wants to observe the other character's response to this revelation, and film maker would almost have to show a close-up of his face.

Otherwise, shot selection in a film is usually determined by the kind of story that is being told. A love story or a psychological study of a character, for example, would be characterized by extensive use of intimate photography (i.e., extreme-close-ups and close-ups); the long shot, or even the medium shot, in this kind of narrative, would tend to erode the feeling of intimacy.

Ingmar Bergman's films, for instance, utilize a great many close-ups and medium-close shots. Bergman's concern, typically, is with an individual or a couple of individuals; consequently, an "intimate" camera is appropriate to his complex, subjective, psychological approach. On the other hand, films which are essentially satirical portraits of society, such as Stanley Kubrick's *Dr. Strangelove,* or Richard Attenborough's *Oh! What a Lovely War* (1969), work at a considerable distance from their characters because Kubrick and Attenborough are depicting types.

An audience's response to an image will also be affected by the speed at which the subject has been photographed. By showing a man running down the street in "fast motion," a film maker can cause the runner to appear ludicrous; but the same man running the same way, photographed in "slow motion," could be made to appear graceful, almost "poetic" in his movements.

Fast motion, which is produced by reducing the speed at which motion is usually photographed, exaggerates the jerkiness and clumsiness of any movement. As a technique, it was a comic staple of the early silent films and it enabled film makers to produce narrow escapes and near accidents without actually endangering anyone's life. Although it is not used as extensively today as it once was, it is still occasionally employed to augment the comedy of a scene as in Tony Richardson's *Tom Jones* (1963), Richard Lester's *The Knack* (1965), and Sam Peckinpah's *The Ballad of Cable Hogue* (1970).

Slow motion, created by increasing the speed at which a subject is normally photographed, renders a dream-like fluidity to motion. As a technique, it is often employed to depict dreams and memories or to "romanticize" or "poeticize" a subject or a setting. One of the concluding scenes of Arthur Penn's *Bonnie and Clyde* (1967) represents a well-known and widely acclaimed example of slow motion photography. The scene referred to is, of course, that in which Bonnie and Clyde are gunned down. In an interview, Penn explained that he employed slow motion in that particular scene in order to impart a "balletic quality" to the film so as to dramatize Bonnie and Clyde's "movement from life to myth".[5]

Thus, it should be clear that the way in which a story is told is at least as important as the story itself. Each of the factors that has been considered in this chapter—point of view, lenses, light, film stock, camera angle and distance—are not mere technical embellishments. They are, in fact, the story itself.

REFERENCES

1. Kazin, Alfred (ed.), *Writers at Work: The Paris Review Interviews: Third Series* (Viking Press, New York, 1967), p. 264.

2. Knight, Arthur, *The Liveliest Art* (New American Library, New York, 1957), p. 158.

3. For an excellent non-technical introduction to the art of cinematography, see Joseph Mascelli's *The Five C's of Cinematography* and Joseph Mercer's *An Introduction to Cinematography*.

4. Stephenson, Ralph and Debrix, J. R., *The Cinema As Art* (Penguin Books, Baltimore, 1965), p. 172.

5. Gelmis, Joseph (ed.), *The Film Director As Superstar* (Doubleday, New York, 1970), p. 222.

Der Führer makes his entrance at the 1933 Nazi-party rally in Nuremburg. Flanking him, at one respectful pace to his rear, are Goering and Goebbels. Those are people lined up on either side of the corridor; they are cheering. This aerial shot is from Leni Riefenstahl's 1934 *Triumph of the Will*.

Courtesy of The Museum of Modern Art/Film Stills Archive

THE ART OF EDITING: STRUCTURE

> One must learn to understand that editing is in actual fact a compulsory and deliberate guidance of the thoughts and associations of the spectator.[1]
>
> V. I. PUDOVKIN

Eisenstein's use of montage during "The Odessa Steps" sequence in *Potemkin* (1925) provides an important insight into the nature of the film experience: The use of time and space in film is very different from time and space as normally perceived.

Courtesy of The Museum of Modern Art/Film Stills Archive

Motion pictures were first exhibited to a paying public by the Lumière Brothers on December 28, 1895, in Paris. This is a shot from one of the numbers on the program, *Train Arriving in a Station.* Initially, the audience panicked— they'd never seen anything like it: As the train approached, it got larger and larger! Only as people grew used to seeing pictures that moved did innovators, such as Melies and Porter, begin to work plot lines into their spectacles.

Courtesy of The Museum of Modern Art/Film Stills Archive

Orson Welles' prolific
use of unusual camera
angles, as here in his
1942 *The Magnificent
Ambersons,* is one of the
trademarks of his
flamboyant style in film
making.

Courtesy of Janus Films, Inc.

The Seventh Seal (1957) exemplifies the stark majesty of Ingmar Bergman's style. Here, the character Death makes his appearance beside a leaden sea.

Courtesy of Janus Films, Inc.

The 1960's saw the emergence of *the film* from that great commercial cradle known as The Movies. Two of the effects of this socio-cultural phenomenon have been the supplanting of the star by the film maker and a resurgence of experimentation among film makers. Here are four views of one of today's leading experimentalists, Stan VanDerBeek.

Courtesy of Stan VanDerBeek, Photo by Bob Hansen.

Federico Fellini is
today's most successful
heir to the Surrealists
of the 1920's and '30's.
Here is a shot from
his 1965 *Juliet of the
Spirits;* it is interesting to
note that in almost
every one of his feature-
length films there is
a reference to the circus
as a metaphor of
life.

Courtesy of Audio Film Center/
Ideal Pictures

Cosmic irony, discussed
in Chapter Five,
operates on the
assumption that fate
actively intervenes
in men's lives, almost
always to their
detriment. No one was
ever more the
victim of fate than
Charlie Chaplin's most
famous character,
The Little Tramp. Here,
we see him in an
early two-reeler entitled
His Trysting Place.
Needless to say, The
Tramp does not
get The Girl.

Courtesy of The Museum of
Modern Art/Film Stills Archive

Note: In the following
film strips the
sequence has been
stepped up for
the sake of clarity.

If a character walks out
of the left-hand side
of the frame, he should
re-enter the next
frame on the right side,
for if he enters from
the left, the audience is
apt to assume that
he has inexplicably
turned around. Directors
hire script girls to
make sure of details like
this for, in the
complexity of the
day-to-day shooting, they
can be easily
overlooked. See page 72.

Courtesy of
Roundtable Films, Inc.
From the film,
Judging People.

The same applies
for a character who
is talking to someone
off-screen; he
has to be facing his
interloquitor.

An example of
fade-out and fade-in.

An example
of a dissolve.

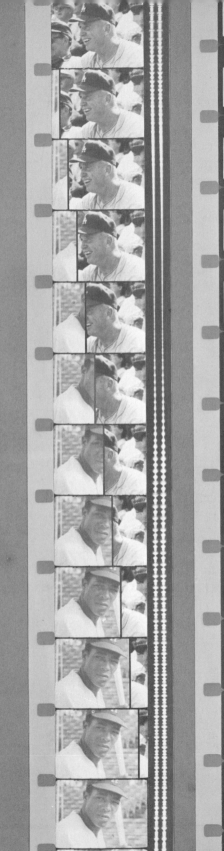

An example
of a wipe.

An example of
split-screen montage.

Courtesy of
Roundtable Films, Inc.
From the film,
Judging People.

RARELY is the novelist or the writer of the short story considered as an editor, for *editor* is a term that is typically restricted to a persons who supervises the production of a newspaper or periodical or to the individual who joins together the various components of the film by a process of cutting, combining and splicing. The word, however, is derived from the Latin word *ēdere* which means to bring forth or to publish. Thus editing could be viewed as a process of selecting, arranging and juxtaposing material in order to bring forth or reveal a subject in the most effective manner.

The problem that confronts the novelist, as well as the film maker, is to find the most dramatic method of revealing his subject. The selection of means is always bound up with the thematic nature of the story.

A novelist, for example, might decide to examine the theme of man's inhumanity to man. This, however, represents an extremely broad spectrum and could be revealed in any number of ways: by examining war, by considering the callous social persecution of ethnic or racial minorities, by revealing the economic exploitation of the poor by the rich. A writer could conceivably attempt to examine all of these situations within the confines of a single novel, but there is a real possibility that depth would be sacrified for scope. Perhaps the writer would decide to limit himself to only two of these possibilities. He thus initiates a process of selection.

Assume that he decides to consider the exploitation of the impoverished racial minorities by the more affluent . . . how is he to do it? Deciding that it would be impossible for him to deal adequately with all of the exploited racial poor of the world, he determines to limit himself to a single class—the poor Blacks of the inner-city ghettos. Once again, he would probably decide to restrict his material, for he is not interested in compiling a statistical abstract of the unbearable conditions of the Black community, but rather he wants to move his reader emotionally, appeal to his sense of compassion and justice. He ultimately decides to use a single family as representative of the entire community.

At each point in the development of this hypothetical novel, the writer has been faced with choices. In each instance, he has attempted to select what he considers to be the most dramatic and emotionally persuasive vehicle for his theme. Even though he has determined what his subject will be, there still remains the problem of how best to reveal this particular family.

The writer decides that he does not want to deal with every aspect of the family's existence from birth to death, but only with those events that deal directly with his theme. Thus, he decides that he needs to restrict his subject even more. He determines to cover a time period of one month.

For the novelist, time is a malleable substance; he is not bound to observe its unfolding in a realistic manner. He might, for instance, decide that he wants to alter the normal flow of time for dramatic purposes. Consequently, he may open his novel by showing the family reduced to abject poverty and despair and use the remainder of his novel to show how their plight came about. Thus, time is altered to serve dramatic purposes. The reader's foreknowledge of the family's fate will certainly affect his response to the story. Even though the family might be enjoying a momentary respite from its bleak existence—an apparent change of fortune or a happy moment—the reader, because of his knowledge of the outcome, will view the incident in an altered perspective.

In the course of writing the novel, the author will also consider ways of heightening the drama of the family's predicament. The writer, for example, might consider the techniques of juxtaposition or of parallel action. Juxtaposition is the technique of placing things in close proximity to each other. A diamond is a beautiful stone in nearly any circumstances, but placed next to a common pebble the exquisite beauty of the diamond is heightened. In the same manner, juxtaposing the meagerness of the Black family's dinner to the comparative lavishness of the typical white, middle-class family's meal dramatically emphasizes the discrepancy between the two races.

Parallel action, on the other hand, usually deals with two different but related actions that are occurring simultaneously. The novelist might include a scene which shows the father of the Black family being turned down for a construction job "because there are no openings at present" and suggest that, at the same time, in another part of the city, a construction foreman is calling the office for additional men because he is so shorthanded that he is behind on the job.

Thus, even though the writer is not thought of as an editor, he must, in the writing of his novel or short story, make a series of decisions that are editorial in nature. The main distinction between the novelist and the film maker as editors lies in the nature of their mediums. The writer deals with words. He assembles his words in a manner (style) that is appropriate to his subject. Obviously, a flippant style would be totally inappropriate to the struggles of the Black family. Through his choice of words and in his description, the writer attempts to convey his theme, and if he has been successful in his choices, the finished novel will be emotionally persuasive—it will move the reader.

Although there are exceptions, the film maker's starting point is usually the film script. In one sense, the film script could be likened to a blueprint, for it enables the film maker to predetermine just what will be required to produce the film; in addition, it apprises the film maker as to what kinds of artistic and technical problems will have to be overcome. The film script should be looked upon as a kind of guide to the film; it is not, of course, the film itself anymore than a map is an actual territory. The film script, on the other hand, is not quite as rigid a document as a map or blueprint; the film maker as he proceeds can make changes in the script, but the builder who ignores the architect's specifications may well find the building tumbling down upon his head.

The actual active raw materials of the film maker, though, are strips of film containing images which, in combination, will ultimately comprise the finished film. The film maker is always faced with the problem of finding a concrete image to convey his meaning. A novelist could write of his character that "he sensed a latent danger in even commonplace events," but the film maker must find concrete visual expressions for this feeling of latent danger. The commonplace cannot be shown as an average person would view it, but through the eyes of a tremendously frightened man. Crossing the street must be revealed as a harrowing experience, strangers on the street must be seen as potential assailants, and innocent acts and gestures perceived as threatening.

The Russian film maker and theoretician, V. I. Pudovkin in his *Film Technique* wrote that "the foundation of film art is *editing*."[2] Later in the same work, he attempted to explain why the editorial process was so critical to the film experience:

> . . . it appears that the active raw material [of the film director] is no other than those *pieces of celluloid* on which, from various view-points, the separate movements of the action have been shot. From nothing but

these pieces is created those appearances upon the screen that form the filmic representation of the action shot. And thus the material of the film director consists not of real processes happening in real space and real time, but those pieces of celluloid on which these processes have been recorded. This celluloid is entirely subject to the will of the director who edits it.[3]

Thus, it would appear that the ultimate "reality" of the film is achieved by the selection, arrangement and juxtaposition of these pieces of celluloid.

For obvious (i.e., financial) reasons, a film is rarely ever shot in sequence. In a studio, there may be a set which was constructed for a particular scene that is used, according to the script, both at the beginning and again at the end of the film. It would be absurd to film the early scene, tear down the set, only to have to reconstruct it again at a later date. Consequently, the later scene will be shot out-of-sequence. The same consideration would hold true for a film that makes use of different locales. Every scene or sequence that takes place in a given locale will be finished there before the company moves on to a new location. This means that not only are most film productions deprived of the kind of continuity that is ordinarily found in the theater, but this method forces the actor to work in a piecemeal fashion. In the theater, the actor would be able to experience a sense of emotional continuity in his role. Sometimes only the director and the script writer are aware of how the completed film will appear to the audience. Sometimes, as in the case of Fellini's, *8½* (1963), only the director knows, and—sometimes—not even the director, as in John Huston's largely improvised *Beat the Devil* (1954).

The completed film, then, is usually six to eight reels (the average length of a reel is 900 to 1200 feet) of exposed film which will ultimately comprise the 90 to 120 minutes that the audience will view on the screen. As a process, editing usually goes through several stages. The film maker, for example, as he is filming the action, could decide on the set that there are several takes (the shots recorded during the production) he knows he doesn't want; an actor could have muffed a line, been temporarily out of character, sneezed, or perhaps a technician wandered onto the set by accident. What the film maker will do is just never have the exposed film processed. Thus, the editing process begins even before the film goes to the cutting room. Once the film does reach the cutting room, the editor puts together the first assembly of the film called the *rough cut*. In the rough cut, the editor selects the best of the takes and joins them together according to the order established by the script. At this point, the film maker confers with the editor in order to further refine the rough cut into the most effective film version which is known as the *fine cut*. Lastly, the supportive material—dialogue, sound, music—is selected and combined in the desired order (this process is referred to as the *mix*) and recorded on the film's sound track. This brief, superficial description of the editing process, however, does not begin to suggest the complexity, the unnumbered decisions and vast amounts of time that go into the editing of a film. There are countless examples of films shot in a couple of weeks that were over a year or more in the editing process. Leni Reifenstahl's film, *Olympia*, for example, described only the events of the 1936 Olympic Games, but it was over a year-and-a-half in editing.[4]

Many writers have suggested that the development of the film art was inextricably bound up with the development of editing. A very brief examination of some of the high points of the development of editing can suggest how the film changed from an interesting experiment to an art form.

Viewed historically,[5] it can be seen that the development of film as an art was in direct relation to its movement away from the conventions of the theater. Many of the turn-of-the-century films—those of the Lumière Brothers, for example—were simply the animations of interesting events; the camera was placed in position, turned on, and subsequently recorded whatever passed in front of its lens. This particular style assumed that the camera was a passive witness to events, that it was the events themselves that provided whatever interest the film would contain. In fact, the only distinguishable difference between this employment of the motion picture camera and the still camera was that the film moved. And, in almost every instance, these early films centered around a single incident.

A short time later, film makers began attempting stories. The films tended to be longer, they did make use of continuity of subject matter, but each scene was distinctly a separate event. In 1902, Thomas Edison's cameraman, Edwin S. Porter, created a short film entitled *The Life of an American Fireman*.[6] Porter's film was unique in several respects: first, it made use of previously existing film footage; second,

Porter managed to suggest the illusion of continuity of action between separate scenes. The audience, for example, would see an exterior shot of a burning building; they watch as the firemen arrive; the film then dissolves to an interior shot of the building showing a mother and child overcome by smoke; the door opens, the fireman enters and carries out the stricken mother. Next, the film dissolves to the exterior of the building to show the mother pleading with the fireman to re-enter the building to save her child. The audience watch while the fireman goes into the building and, after a few moments, comes out with the child cradled in his arms. Porter's use of existing material suggested that the "reality" of the film experience was derived not so much from the action photographed, but from the joining together of the strips of celluloid. In viewing the film, the audience was not able to tell the difference between the already existing footage and the footage that had been shot expressly for the film. Porter also demonstrated that if illusion of continuity could be achieved by the skillful juxtaposition of shots, the audience would accept the transitions as credible.

Despite Porter's important contributions, the camera still remained anchored to its fixed position. In the next few years, however, some significant changes took place in the narration of films. By 1915, D. W. Griffith, in his *The Birth of a Nation,* was making use of numerous technical innovations: The camera was moving from wide panoramic shots to close-ups; areas of the screen image were selectively darkened (masked) for dramatic emphasis; the overall action was fragmented into components (long shots, close-ups, etc.) and the finished scene reconstructed from these components; the timing of shots was being employed for dramatic purposes—rapid cutting, for example, was used to suggest the exhilaration of a chase. By Griffith's time, the film had made several radical departures from the conventions of the stage. The use of the close-up not only increased the film maker's control over his audience's response, but it also gave rise to a new style of acting that was much more restrained than the acting style of the theater. The fragmentation of a scene introduced an unprecedented depiction of reality. The timing of the length of a shot made it possible for the film maker to influence his viewers' emotional reaction to a given scene. Movement of the camera exchanged the artifical frontal perspective of the theater for the more realistic experience of shifting perspective found in film.

By 1925, Russian film makers such as Sergei Eisenstein and V. I. Pudovkin had developed the philosophy of *montage*.[7] Montage is a process of creative editing whereby the images derive their meaning from juxtaposition with other images. Eisenstein, for example, explained that the continuity of a film should be created by a series of shocks and conflicts, and that it is the splicing of images that produces the conflict. Montage has also been employed to compress time. For example, rather than showing a man emerge from a cab, walk to the door of a building, enter the lobby, press the elevator button, wait, enter the elevator, ascend to the fifth floor, enter the hall and proceed to his office, the film maker need only to show the man leave the cab, then cut to him entering the building, and finally cut to him pushing open the door to his office. The audience watching this latter sequence will assume that the actor has gone through all the intervening steps even though they haven't actually witnessed them. Montage can also be used to produce the opposite effect —the expansion of time.

In the famous "Odessa Steps" sequence in *The Battleship Potemkin* (1926), Eisenstein shows a force of Cossacks marching down the steps slaughtering the citizens of Odessa who have gathered there. By constantly moving back and forth from the descent of the Cossacks to the reactions of the stricken and terrified people, Eisenstein actually elongates time. In other words, the running time of the film is actually much longer than it would take the Cossacks, in "real" time, to descend the steps.

Eisenstein's use of montage during the "Odessa Steps" sequence provides an important insight into the nature of the film experience: The use of time and space in film is very different from time and space as normally perceived. Eisenstein's purpose is not to depict the actual passage of time realistically, but to portray it dramatically. By elongating time, he has succeeded in heightening the drama of the incident. This is simply another way of saying that time varies in its dramatic intensity and, in this respect, it is a matter of common sense to devote more film time to the dramatically important events and less to the insignificant.

A hypothetical example might serve to point up how a film maker goes about manipulating time. A man arises, brushes his teeth, eats breakfast while reading the newspaper, and exchanges a few words of conversation with his wife. He dresses, leaves his home and walks to the street corner. The bus arrives and he boards. The driver is surly because the man does not have the right amount of change. The man rides to work reading the newspaper. He leaves the bus and walks a block to his office. Upon entering the building, he boards the elevator and, after a few moments, disembarks and walks to his office. As he enters the office, he says hello to the secretaries and then proceeds to his desk; he hears muffled laughter behind him. Seated at his desk, he begins to work on the papers piled up before him. He drops one of the papers, bends down to pick it up and notices that, in his hurry to leave home in the morning, he had put on two different shoes. He experiences embarrassment. The remainder of the morning, he works at his desk. Still feeling embarrassed about the shoes, he remains at his desk through the lunch hour. His stomach begins to growl. Later in the afternoon, he is called into the manager's office and chewed out because of a miscalculation in one of the papers he had handled. Humiliated, he takes the paper and returns to his desk whereupon he discovers that the error is not his. He calls the guilty party to his desk. The other person, unperturbed by the incident, shrugs it off by saying, "Well, everyone makes mistakes," and promptly returns to his desk. Five o'clock, and the man leaves the office, retracing the route he had taken that morning. He arrives at the bus stop just in time to see his bus, a few seconds early, pulling away from the curb. It begins to drizzle and he has to wait twenty minutes in the rain. After he arrives home, his wife casually asks him if he had remembered to pay the light bill while he was in town, and the man explodes in fury.

The sheer length of this example should suggest that many superfluities have been included. It is unlikely that an audience would be interested in the man brushing his teeth, eating breakfast, riding the bus, walking to work, handling the papers, and returning home. The audience "knows" all this already; consequently, the film maker can eliminate these events as being dramatically unimportant. What is important about the scene is the series of frustrating events which ultimately produce the angry explosion that occurs when the man arrives home. These incidents make the outburst both natural and credible.

The film maker would probably eliminate the intervening undramatic events in order to concentrate on the frustrating incidents. This could probably be accomplished in five minutes of film time. Since the audience is fully prepared for the scene which takes place when the man arrives home, it would be legitimate for the film maker to elongate this incident because it represents the natural culmination of his dramatic build-up; it is more important than the minor dramatic incidents that precede it. In this example, time serves a dramatic rather than a realistic master.

Film is capable of altering not only time but space as well. V. I. Pudovkin, in his *Film Technique,* pointed out that Eisenstein's "Odessa Steps" episode was shot in three different geographical locations.[8] The battleship was filmed at Odessa, but the stone lions which appear in this scene are located in the Crimea, and the iron gates are in Moscow. Thus the location that appears in this scene does not exist in actuality. By the relatively simple act of joining strips of film, the film maker is capable of creating virtually any kind of spatial relationship that he desires. The film maker could, for example, show the audience a frontal view of a rustic mountain cabin in the Smokies. The viewer would see the mountain scene flanking the cabin. Inside the cabin, the camera shows the occupant walking towards a window in the rear of the cabin. The camera, in close-up, shows the occupant looking out of the window. The audience sees what he sees—the Sahara Desert! The example, of course, is farfetched, but it does point up that film is capable of accomplishing such a feat. The film maker is not bound to mechanically reproduce reality as he finds it, but the film maker rarely ever alters time and space without a valid reason—the changes he introduces will always be related to meaning.

Another aspect of the editing process that is intimately related to meaning is the *rhythm* of a film. Unfortunately, the discussion of rhythm in relation to art is frequently limited to music alone. But it is obvious that life is filled with rhythmical patterns: the very act of breathing, the beating of the heart, the passage of a day, the changing of the seasons, the rotation of the earth. It is also clear that rhythm is related to meaning: A rapid increase in breathing is usually related to excitement, a rise in the rate of the heart beat may be prompted by anxiety and fear. Although few students of poetry would fail to consider the relation of rhythm to meaning in a poem, many students of film overlook the contribution that rhythm can make to a film.

Basically, a film deals with two kinds of rhythm: *internal rhythm,* the rhythm that is being conveyed within the shot itself (a shot of a man strolling would depict a slow internal rhythm, whereas the same man running would obviously depict an increase in the tempo of the rhythm); and *external rhythm*, which is the actual length of time a given shot remains on the screen (a series of very brief one-second shots would impart a fast external rhythm to a scene, whereas shots that ran a couple of minutes in length could be described in terms of a slow external rhythm). Rhythm, like everything that the film maker does, supports and intensifies meaning.

In many ways, the rhythm of a scene corresponds to the way in which a person would ordinarily perceive a scene. If a person were standing in a room watching four men seated at a table playing cards, the scene would probably move relatively slowly. The eyes of the observer would blink at a normal rhythm, the action would shift slowly from one player to another. However, if the game were to erupt into a brawl, there would be a simultaneous increase of tempo and movement. The film maker would attempt to approximate the responses of the observer by decreasing the length of the cuts. The shift from the slow-moving cuts of the card playing to the rapid chaotic cuts of the fight would approximate the viewer's reaction to such a scene.

On the other hand, to employ quick cuts in a scene which is generally quiet and peaceful would be very inappropriate because the rapidity of the cuts would fight the emotional content of the scene. This is not to suggest that every quiet scene will employ "slow" cuts and every exciting scene "fast" cuts. What does determine the pace of the scene is the emotional effect that the film maker is trying to evoke. For example, the curling of smoke is generally a slow, languorous, lazy movement, but if the film maker is trying to suggest that various chemical elements that smoke throws into our atmosphere are polluting our environment at an alarming rate, he would want to visually modify the normal depiction of rising smoke. He might show a quick cut of smoke billowing out of a car's exhaust, cut to a truck's exhaust, to a jet plane, to an incinerator, and, finally, to a slow-burning garbage dump. If the film maker cuts from shot to shot quickly enough, the viewer not only receives the impression that the pollution is spreading at an alarming rate, but he will also sense, because of the very speed at which the images are moving, that the whole problem of pollution has somehow gotten out of control. In other words, through the use of accelerated external rhythm and juxtaposition, the film maker was able to create concepts that represent more than the sum of the original materials.

In the above example, a rapid external technique was imposed upon material with a basically slow internal rhythm in order to make a serious point. The very same technique can also be utilized to create comic or satiric effects. It could be argued, for example, that everything possesses its own particular rhythm and performs varying activities at different rhythms: people walk in a recognizable rhythm, plants grow in certain rhythms. To alter the normal rhythm of an activity is literally to force a viewer to perceive its meaning differently. Baking a cake, for example, is ordinarily a slow methodical process. However, if the film maker were to impose a rapid external rhythm on the activities taking place in the kitchen, the baking process would take on an absurd, frantic and nonsensical dimension. If the film maker wished to exaggerate this effect even more, he might decide to film the action in fast motion, in which case he would be combining a rapid internal rhythm with a fast external rhythm. *Laugh-In,* the award winning television show, bases many of its sight gags on just this type of technique. Similarly, in novels and plays, comic exchanges are usually characterized by brevity and a simultaneous increase in tempo.

External rhythm is largely a mechanical one that is created by the duration of a shot, whereas internal rhythm partakes of a more natural rhythm arising from within the scene itself. In cutting a film, however, the film maker must take into consideration many other factors as well. The cuts, except in the instances where the film maker is trying to produce an unusual effect, should proceed naturally and intelligibly. If a character who is standing to the left of a frame looking towards the left should speak to another character out-of-frame, the audience naturally looks for the other character's response. The other character will probably be shown, in the following shot, standing to the right of the frame, looking right, towards the character who has just spoken. However, if he is shown in the same position as the first speaker, the two shots are apt to be very confusing. Likewise, if a character walks out of the left-hand side of the frame, he should re-enter the next frame on the right side, for if he enters from the left side, the audience is apt to assume that he has inexplicably turned around.

The film maker should anticipate the audience's response to a shot, and, in most instances, fulfill its expectations. For example, the film maker might show two characters seated across the room from each other conversing. One character suddenly makes a surprising, rather serious accusation. The audience naturally wants to view the other person's response. Clearly, a close-up would be called for in the next shot. Likewise, if the film maker shows two characters walking down the street engrossed in a lively conversation, then cuts to a close-up of an open manhole, the audience will begin to anticipate one of the men falling in. This does not mean that the film maker must have one of the characters fall in, for he could just as easily have a worker rise up in the manhole at just the right moment to provide a stepping stone, but the point is that the film maker virtually has to make some use of the manhole.

By the same token, his shots should be intelligible to the audience. If the film maker shows a billboard or a letter, there should be enough time for the audience to read it. In general, the audience should have more time to comprehend a long shot than a close-up, for the long shot takes more time to perceive. The audience should also know where a scene is taking place. Arbitrarily to move an audience from one location to another without indicating the shift in locale is unnecessarily disorienting. Along the same lines, an audience will need more time to comprehend the new location, object, or character.

The film maker should always have a reason for employing a cut and there should be either a thematic or visual relationship between cuts. Changing the image simply for the sake of providing another, different one can be of little value.

The cut is simply one way of moving from one image to another. In general, the use of a cut in a film suggests that there has been no break in the action, that the movement of the scene is continuous. There are, however, many other ways of providing transitions between shots and scenes. Many of these techniques are introduced during the editing process.

The *fade* was once a rather common transitional device in film making. Basically, there are two different kinds: the *fade-in,* in which the viewer sees a totally black screen, then watches the screen gradually lighten to reveal an image, and the *fade-out,* in which the viewer observes the lighted image darken to a black screen. Because the fade is of longer duration than the cut, it has the effect of breaking the flow of action, separating, as it were, one scene from the next. Consequently, the fade not only retards time, but it also gives the audience an opportunity to momentarily consider the preceding scene.

The *dissolve,* like the fade, does not enjoy the currency it once did, but it is still used occasionally as a transitional device. A dissolve gradually merges two different images. For example, the audience might be looking at the skyline of New York then gradually become aware of yet another image, a view of Paris, behind the New York skyline. The New York skyline disappears, leaving only the Parisian scene. The implication is that the scene of action has shifted from New York to Paris. The dissolve is sometimes used in films to introduce and terminate flashback sequences.

The *super* or *super-imposure* is very close to the dissolve, the only difference being that both shots are held on the screen simultaneously. What happens is that two shots are printed on top of each other so that when they are projected on the screen, the viewer sees both of them at the same time. The super has the effect of suggesting that two separate but related actions are occurring at the same time. By showing an audience an image of a burning building superimposed on an image of a fire truck racing to the rescue, the film maker indicates that both activities are happening simultaneously.

Another technique that has lately come into fashion to indicate simultaneous action is *split-screen montage.* In this instance, the screen is divided up into separate areas. Each area of the screen shows a separate but related activity. For example, it is conceivable that a fire scene could be handled by this technique. The film maker could split the screen into five areas. In one section, he could show the exterior of the burning building; in another, a woman trapped inside the building being overcome by smoke; in another section, a man poised in one of the windows of the building working up enough courage to jump; a fourth section could show firemen smashing in the door of the building with axes, while the fifth might show the fire chief, on his two-way radio, calling for additional assistance.

Two other transitional techniques that are not in much use today are the *flip* and the *wipe,* though the flip is still used fairly extensively in TV, a medium which, through the economic challenge it poses, has freed today's film from many of its former restrictions and taboos. In the wipe, the viewers witnesses one shot changing to another by means of a moving line which usually travels from side to side, or from the top to the bottom of the frame. As the line moves across the image, it simultaneously "wipes out" the old image and reveals the new one. The flip is a slight modification of the wipe, for the image appears to roll over, revealing another image; typically, the rotation is on either a vertical or horizontal axis. At present, most film makers tend to avoid the flip and the wipe; the consensus of feeling seems to be that the cut, fade, and dissolve provide more "natural" visual transitions than the flip or the wipe. Today, indeed, the cut has become the paramount transitional device.

It is also rare to see a current film maker employing the *mask,* although it was a favorite device of D. W. Griffith. Basically, the mask darkens selected areas of the image in order to produce a special visual effect. Using the mask, the film maker can render the impression of how a shot might appear through binoculars, a periscope, or a keyhole. Griffith, for instance, used a device called the "iris" whereby he would darken the frame except for a small circular area in the center; he would then "open up" the iris to reveal the entire scene.

Although film makers make use of nearly all the editorial techniques mentioned above, their films tend to be remarkably different experiences. After witnessing only a few minutes of a Welles, a Bergman or a Fellini film, the viewer is acutely aware that he is dealing with three quite different sensibilities. This awareness proceeds from the recognition of readily distinguishable differences in the three films: differences in subject matter, differences in approach and, particularly, differences in the presentation of visual images—in fact, with three different styles. Style, of course, is not merely a technique that is arbitrarily imposed upon the material, but rather a method that is indigenous to the story.

Although there are virtually as many different styles as there are film makers, it is possible to distinguish between two very general stylistic approaches: *continuity editing* and *dynamic editing.*

In general, continuity editing attempts to portray the action of a story in a "realistic" manner, that is, the emphasis is on the creation of a smooth, continuous flow of events. In many respects, this technique could be likened to the experience of the theater, for the depiction of the story, its movement and dialogue tend to proceed in a predictable, continuous line. This style of editing will usually tend to make use of long, uninterrupted stretches of action. For example, if the film maker were attempting to film the traditional chase scene of the western by means of continuity editing, he would, in all probability, remain with only one of the two parties. The audience would tend to identify with the heroes; consequently, the film maker would reveal the chase from their point of view. If the pursued are the heroes, the pursuers would always be viewed from the pursued's vantage point. Although it might appear that this technique would result in a static chase, this is not always the case. Director George Roy Hill, in *Butch Cassidy and the Sun Dance Kid,* used this technique with great dramatic effect. Paul Newman and Robert Redford undergo a number of increasingly difficult ordeals in order to "shake off" a posse that is after them, dead or alive. They use every trick in the book to throw their nameless, relentless pursuers off their track . . . to no avail. Newman's despairing wail, "Who *are* those guys?" provides one of the serio-comic highlights of the 1970 film season.

A more conventional way of depicting the chase sequence, though, is by means of dynamic editing. In this instance, the viewer would see a medium shot of the heroes galloping across the plains and, immediately afterward witness, in another medium shot, the villains in pursuit. Dynamic editing disregards "realistic" spatial relationships in order to concentrate on the drama of the chase; it is clear that the juxtaposition of the two medium shots of the heroes and the villains has no counterpart in normal spatial relationships.

Dynamic editing usually proceeds by the technique of fragmenting the story into carefully selected pieces of action. In this style of editing, the emphasis shifts to relational contrasts. Often this form of editing can give rise to responses which are more in the eye of the beholder than in the film itself. In an experiment, Russian director V. I. Pudovkin and film theoretician L. V. Kuleshov[9] recorded some footage of an actor with a completely neutral expression. They then cut up this footage and interspersed it with shots of a bowl of soup, a shot of a coffin containing a woman, and another shot of a young girl playing with a toy. When the film was projected, the audience was impressed by the actor's subtle acting style. They "saw" him expressing longing at the bowl of soup, grief at the loss of the woman, and joy when he perceived the young girl at play. Clearly, it was the juxtaposition of the shots, rather than their inherent value, that created the meaning.

The entire philosophy of montage developed by Eisenstein and

Pudovkin is very much in accord with the principles of dynamic editing. It could even be argued that the development of dynamic editing was one of the main factors in freeing the film from the slavish imitation of theatrical techniques. Today, it is rare to see a film maker create an entire film which is exclusively devoted to one of these editing styles; more typically, the two styles are used in combination to help create a logical rhythm for the film itself.

It might be asked that if most film makers make use of continuity editing as well as dynamic editing, how then is an individual style achieved in a film? Although it may sound facetious to say so, ultimately, the style of the individual film maker is determined by the culmination of virtually everything that has occurred in the film. It was suggested earlier that the subject matter of the film must be considered. The viewer must evaluate what landscape the film maker has decided to explore: the relationships that exist between individuals, the effect of society upon the individual, or is it a larger canvas?—perhaps the sweeping events of history? Obviously, the choice of social, historical and physical landscapes determine to a great extent how the story will be handled. What kind of attitude does the film maker take towards his material? Is he objective, scornful, sardonic, satiric, bemused, reverent, remorseful? More importantly, how does he realize the story? Does he work in black and white or in color? Does either medium possess special characteristics? Is it rich, garish, grainy, dull or bright? How are the shots and scene presented visually? Are they cluttered and busy, or are they stark and motionless? What kind of angles, lenses and editing techniques are employed? What contribution does the sound make? How fast or how slow do the images move? Who are the actors, and how are they revealed? It might appear that these questions are directed toward what the film is about, but what the film is *about* is an abstraction. It could be *about* man's inhumanity to man, *about* love, *about* injustice; what it's about is not necessarily what it *means*, however. If you comprehend the style of the film, you, at the same time, grasp its how, for the style is the how.

Thus far, the elements and techniques of editing have been dealt with in a piecemeal, abstract fashion. At this point, it might be useful to examine a portion of a hypothetical script which involves a single scene. By so doing, it can be demonstrated how the editor goes about selecting material, why he selects what he does, and how the joining of these strips of celluloid affects the response of the viewer.

The scene outlined below describes a fugitive who goes to a public park to meet a "friend." The friend, however, has informed the police of the forthcoming meeting and the park has been staked out. Dialogue and sound have been eliminated in order to concentrate on the impact of the visuals. The numbers to the right of the shot description indicate in seconds the running time of each shot (approximately one-and-one-half-feet of film are projected every second.)

E.L.S./extreme long shot; L.S./long shot; M.L.S./medium long shot; M.S./medium shot; M.C.U./medium close-up; C.U./close-up; E.C.U./extreme close-up.

Shot description	Running time of shot in seconds
1. M.S. of fugitive in an apartment, standing before a mirror buckling on a shoulder holster. He looks to the left. cut to (all transitions between shots are cuts unless otherwise indicated:)	20
2. C.U. Clock on the table: three-thirty	2
3. M.S. Fugitive walks to door of apartment and opens door into the hall.	10
4. M.S. Door of a bus opening inward and fugitive boarding bus. He deposits fare and moves toward the back of the bus.	20
5. M.C.U. Fugitive seated beside an older woman dressed in black. Buildings, store fronts, pedestrians, etc., are visible through the windows of the bus. The bus moves from right to left.	30

Shot description	Running time of shot in seconds
6. L.S. Reverse Angle (i.e., the viewers sees this scene from the opposite angle as previous shot). Group of people standing on corner. Bus comes into frame from left side and discharges passengers. Fugitive gets off. Park can be seen in the background.	15
7. M.S. Fugitive at entrance of the park purchasing newspaper from a vendor.	10
8. M.C.U. Fugitive seated at park bench reading paper. Looks at wrist watch.	5
9. E.C.U. Wrist watch: four o'clock.	3
10. M.S. Fugitive lighting a cigarette as he continues to read the paper.	10
11. C.U. Paper on the ground beside the park bench.	3
12. M.S. Fugitive dropping cigarette on ground and grinding it out with his foot. Looks in the direction of the park entrance.	10
13. L.S. Park entrance. Couple walks in holding hands.	10

Dissolve to:

14. C.U. Fugitive's foot grinding out another cigarette. There is the litter of a half dozen cigarettes lying on the ground.	8
15. L.S. Man rising and beginning to pace back and forth in front of the park bench.	20

	Running time of shot in seconds
Shot description	
16. C.U. Park pigeon pacing nervously.	10
17. M.S. Fugitive sitting down again; looks at watch.	12
18. E.C.U. Wrist watch: five o'clock.	3
19. L.S. Park entrance--light beginning to fail--couple with their arms around each other departing.	15
20. M.S. Fugitive seated at park bench. Picks up discarded paper.	10
21. C.U. Newspaper; page is open to a travel ad.	8

Dissolve to:

22. M.S. (High contrast) Fugitive dressed in expensive clothes; he stands on the balcony of what looks to be a lavish hotel. The door opens behind him and an attractive woman, carrying a drink on a tray appears. She places the tray on a table. He puts a cigarette to his lips. She deliberately picks up a lighter, lights it, and begins to bring the light towards his cigarette.	25

Dissolve to:

23. M.S. Fugitive back on park bench, cigarette dangling from mouth. Hand comes into frame holding a light.	8

| | Running time of shot in seconds |
Shot description	
24. C.U. Fugitive's face; look of surprise and fear, followed by recognition.	5
25. C.U. of man who lit cigarette. His face is tense and his eyes slowly shift right.	7
26. C.U. of fugitive turning his eyes in the same direction.	6
27. L.S. Large bush near park entrance; man standing behind the bush.	5
28. C.U. Same shot as #25. Man's eyes shift left.	6
29. L.S. Man, dressed in conservative business suit, sitting on a park bench reading a newspaper.	5
30. Same shot as #25. Man's eyes look upward.	6
31. E.L.S. Roof of a building facing park. A figure is seen silhouetted against the sky.	8
32. M.S. Fugitive jumps up and rushes from bench; camera pans with him as he runs into the bushes.	5
33. L.S. Man on park bench drops newspaper, jumps up, pulling out a pistol as he does, and begins to run toward the camera.	7
34. L.S. Man runs out from behind bush near park entrance. He holds a gun in his hand and runs toward the camera.	6

Shot description	Running time of shot in seconds
35. E.L.S. Figure on roof top raises small radio to his lips.	8
36. M.S. Police switchboard operator seen talking and pushing plugs into switchboard.	6
37. L.S. Police squad car driving away from camera, stops abruptly, turns around and heads back in the direction of the camera.	10
38. Super M.S. of motorcycle cop starting his cycle. C.U. of interior of squad car, one officer talking on two-way radio.	5
39. M.S. Fugitive running through bushes.	6
40. M.S. Plainclothes detective running through bushes.	4
41. M.L.S. Motorcycle cop approaching park.	3
42. L.S. Squad car coming to an abrupt stop at another corner of the park.	2
43. E.C.U. Fugitive, now breathing heavily, still running.	5

This scene, or some variation on it, has been seen countless times on the screen; it represents a basic ingredient of the "Cops and Robbers" films. Nonetheless, it does illustrate most of the basic elements of the editing process.

First, notice what has happened to time. The events, described here took, in "real" time, about two-and-one-half hours to occur, but the screen version lasts about four-and-one-half minutes. Thus, two-and-one-half hours are squeezed into less than five minutes. The film maker is able to do this by eliminating what is unessential to his purposes. Rather than giving the viewer a detailed transcription of all the events, he merely sketches in the outlines of the action. For example, the cut from shot #3 to #4 not only eliminates the fugitive's journey from his apartment to the bus stop but also his wait at the stop. The shot, however, is connected by means of similar distances from the subject (they are both medium shots) and the connected movements of the apartment door and door of the bus. Likewise, shot #14 accomplishes a similar purpose by showing the accumulation of cigarette butts on the ground—the viewer assumes that the fugitive has been waiting long enough to have smoked that many cigarettes. In a much more obvious fashion, the close-ups of the clock and the wrist watch indicate passage of time. They are not arbitrary, though, for they indicate the fugitive's nervousness and impatience.

A quick glance at the time alotted to each shot will indicate that the time a shot is permitted to remain on the screen is directly related to the pace of the action. The early parts of the screen describe a slow internal movement, consequently, the duration of the shots is longer. But, in the latter part of the scene, the internal movement accelerates during the chase, and the shots of briefer duration emphasize that excitement.

Some of the shots also provide the viewer with certain visual clues as to what is going to occur. When the fugitive is on the bus in shot #5, a certain ominousness is created by having him seated next to the widow dressed in black. In the park (shot #16), the script makes use of a film simile that not only parodies the fugitive's movements (the nervous jerky movements of the pigeon is analogous to the fugitive's pacing), but also comments upon his plight—having been set up by the informer, he is, literally, a "pigeon."

Most of the transitions used in this scene are cuts. Their use suggests that the action is continuous. In three instances, however, the script calls for dissolves. The first dissolve, which precedes shot #14, is used to suggest the passage of time. Dissolves two and three, before and after shot #22), however, serve to introduce and conclude the escape fantasy that the fugitive has while he is waiting in the park. Notice also the transitions that are used to link the fantasy to reality. The travel ad in the newspaper suggests the idea of the fantasy and the lighting of the cigarette concludes it.

Not only does this scene alter time, but it also manipulates space.

This is particularly true towards the conclusion of the scene when the script calls for a series of shots (#35 through #38) that are widely separated spatially.

The editing style used in the scene makes use of continuity editing (roughly the first half of the script) in the portions of the script which employ a relatively static point of view and emphasize continuity. The latter half of the scene, however, brings in dynamic editing principles; the emphasis shifts from continuity to dramatic emphasis; this portion of the script also makes use of a montage sequence (shots #25 through #43).

This script makes very little use of special visual effects. In shot #38, a "super" is employed to suggest the simultaneous coordinated activities of the police throughout the city. It is possible that a similar effect could be obtained by use of the split-screen montage; it would have had the effect of heightening the number of activities that the police were involved in, but it would have, at the same time, introduced an "unnatural" visual technique into a film which is predominantly a "realistic" depiction of action.

Finally, it should be noticed that nearly every shot in the script contains an element of continuity that transfers to the following shot. In shot #25, for example, the man's eyes turn to the right and, in the following shot, the fugitive sees what the man is looking at—the detective who is partially hidden behind the bush. Likewise, in shot #35, the policeman who is stationed on the roof of the building raises the two-way radio to his lips and, in the succeeding shot, the audience sees who he is speaking to—the police switchboard operator.

The success or failure of this scene is greatly dependent upon the events preceding it. If the audience is aware that the fugitive has been set up by the informer, then nearly every activity of the scene will contain elements of latent danger. On the other hand, if the audience is not forewarned of the trap, there will certainly be present the element of surprise, but parts of the scene might now appear to be static and boring.

Contemporary cinema appears to be moving towards a richer, denser depiction of experience. Having at last freed itself from the conventions of the theater, film has begun to take advantage of the uniqueness of its medium. Conventional editorial techniques of transitions and continuity are slowly being abandoned in favor of a more elliptical style of film making. The pace of films has accelerated considerably; it is very common today to witness films which make use of cuts that verge on the subliminal but, amazingly, the viewer is able to grasp and understand what he has seen. Split-screen montage presents the viewer with as many as a dozen separate but related images and still the viewer is capable of perceiving them all at the same time. Today's experimentalists frequently make use of multiple screens in order to create a more unique viewing experience. Without benefit of a camera or recording equipment, images as well as soundtracks have been applied directly to the film strip.

The unprecedented amount of experimentation that is taking place in film today is a sign of vigorous, exciting medium. The contributions of the innovators eventually find their way back to the narrative film and the result is a more unique and moving film experience.

REFERENCES

1. Pudovkin, V. I., *Film Technique and Film Acting* (Vision Press, Hackensack, 1958), p. 73.

2. *Ibid.,* p. 23.

3. *Ibid.* p. 84.

4. Sarris, Andrew (ed.), *Interviews with Film Directors* (Bobbs-Merrill, New York, 1957), p. 398.

5. For an excellent overview of both the history of editing as well as a fine introduction to the editorial art, see Karel Reisz' *The Technique of Film Editing* (Focal Press, New York, 1958).

6. For a more detailed description of Porter's *The Life of an American Fireman* see Lewis Jacobs' *The Rise of the American Film* (Harcourt, Brace and Co., New York, 1939).

7. Most of Eisenstein's observations on film theory can be found in his two volumes *The Film Sense* and *Film Form* (Meridian Books, New York, 1942 and 1949).

8. Pudovkin, p. 117.

9. *Ibid.,* p. 169.

When audiences actually heard Al Jolson singing *Mammy,* they were also hearing the death knell for the so-called silent era of films. Here is a shot from the first "talkie," Warner Brothers' 1927 *The Jazz Singer.*

Courtesy of The Museum of Modern Art/Film Stills Archive

From the opening sequence of Alain Resnais' *Hiroshima Mon Amour* (1959).

Courtesy of Audio Film Center/ Ideal Pictures

APPEAL TO THE EAR:

SOUND

❝ Life is inseparable from sound. ❞
SIEGFRIED KRACAUER[1]

DESPITE the fact that the addition of sound was the single most important technical innovation in film in almost thirty years, it caused the film, as an art form, to revert to a stage of crudity that was paralleled only by the first of the silent films. When Warner Brothers released their first "talkie," *The Jazz Singer* with Al Jolson, in the latter part of 1927, the death knell for the so-called silent era had been tolled.[2]

The enthusiasm for pictures that talked was almost as great as the earlier enthusiasm for pictures that moved. By 1929, a little over a year after the release of *The Jazz Singer,* nearly every major motion picture in the United States talked. The motivation prompting the rapid conversion to sound was fairly obvious: Paid admissions to the theaters, by 1929, had nearly doubled. The "talkies" were clearly ascendent, the "silents" eclipsed.

The term "silents," however, as a descriptive label for thirty years of movie making is somewhat misleading, for it suggests that early audiences viewed films that were totally devoid of sound. But completely silent films were the exception rather than the rule. Nearly every important motion picture, as well as a large percentage of less significant films, utilized some sort of musical score. For example, D. W. Griffith's *Birth of a Nation,* which was first shown to audiences in February 1915, utilized an original symphonic score by Joseph Carl Breil and an orchestra of 70 musical instruments. Even in "smaller" theaters, it was common practice for a trio of musicians to provide musical accompaniment for early films. However, prior to the entry of the "talkies," many theaters began to replace the musicians with an organist who accompanied the film on the recently developed Wurlitzer organ. Even today, an occasional Wurlitzer can still be seen in some of the older and larger theaters.

The use of music during the silent era was prompted by both practical and aesthetic considerations. As might be expected, a gathering of people is usually a noisy affair: patrons shifted in their seats, scraped their chairs, coughed and talked. In addition to the clamor of the audience, there was the machinery of the early projectors to contend with which produced an audible and distracting whirring sound. Musical accompaniment, in part, resolved these intrusive sounds by providing a backdrop of sound that not only muted undesirable noises but also had the effect of welding a collection of individuals into a unified audience.

But the use of music is not to be explained away by describing it in terms of a blanket of sound. Siegfried Kracauer, in his *Theory of Film,* pointed out that the music remained even though the noisy projectors were removed from the theater and placed in soundproof projection rooms.[3]

For some time silent film makers had been attracted to music because they recognized the dramatic potentialities inherent in it Music, it was clear, had the capability of creating an atmosphere, suggesting an emotion (joy, fear, grief, triumph), or adding an additional dimension of meaning by counterpointing a visual image with a musical score with a totally different emotional value. For example, the screen might reveal an important, dignified character carrying out some serious task yet the racy musical accompaniment suggests that the character's actions are pompous and comic. Music, as might be expected, was relatively unaffected by the coming of sound. It bridged the transition from silent to sound films to become an even more integral aspect of the film experience.

Although the advent of sound, in retrospect, seems to be abrupt and unheralded, it had been in the offing for a long time. Even before the turn of the twentieth century, there had already been several successful short talking films produced in Europe. In America, Thomas Alva Edison's continued experimentation with the sound film was spurred primarily by his desire to find a device that would produce images to accompany his "talking" machine, the Victrola.

But more important than the novelty value of pictures that talked was the ability of sound to correct many of the obvious artistic shortcomings that were inherent in the films of the silent era.

The most apparent advantage of sound was that it enabled the film maker to eliminate the subtitles and captions of the silent film. The subtitle, of course, was the printed narration or dialogue that was flashed on the screen between the scenes. Their disadvantages were numerous. First, they represented a jarring interruption in the succession of the visual images, making it nearly impossible for the film maker to establish and maintain a subtle rhythmic flow. Second, there was nearly always a marked incongruity between the visual images and the linguistic transcription contained in the subtitle. For example, there is an undeniable element of humor produced in watching a couple ranting and raving at each other for several minutes then reading the laconic observation: "They part in anger." Finally, it is clear that subtitles produced a process of duplication that significantly slowed down the movement and development of action.*

As Ralph Stephenson and J. R. Debrix suggest: "The introduction of sound freed the image to be itself, in other words, relieved it of the need to try and express sounds in visual terms."[4] From the inception of the silent film, film makers had had to struggle with the problem of finding visual equivalents for sounds. Cutting from a shot of a gossipy ladies luncheon to a shot of a gaggle of geese adequately conveys the atmosphere of the luncheon by means of a film metaphor but, at the same time, the unique quality of the luncheon is lost. With sound, the film maker was much better equipped to create a stronger sense of factual reality.

The sound film also made it possible for the film maker to extend the boundaries of the screen beyond what was actually seen. In the days of the silent film, if a film maker wished to portray the gossipy ladies' luncheon described in the previous paragraph, he would have had to film the majority of the action by means of medium-long shots; visually this would convey the desired effect of many women speaking at once. On the other hand, with sound, this would not be necessary. He could pick out, in close-up, two ladies who best characterized the stereotyped gossips; their conversation could dominate the foreground of sound, while microphones recorded other conversations for background sound. Though the viewer is only watching two women, he is simultaneously aware, through the sound track, of the presence of all the other women.

In addition to enlarging the scene of action, sound also enabled the film maker to increase the density of the film experience. There is something incongruous about watching a character standing on a busy corner in New York City in a silent film. The accompaniment of sound—the noises of the city streets—would not only enrich the reality of this scene but would also convey a strong sense of place, enabling the film maker to build up the detail of a given scene without having to show the viewer the source of every sound.

The addition of sound caused the film to become both technically and artistically a far more complex medium. That sound would create

---

*Another disadvantage of subtitles was the annoyance of hearing someone in the audience ask, "What did it say?"

an abundance of technical problems almost goes without saying, but the development of sound was simultaneously accompanied by more subtle and complex delineation of character. During the silent era, a psychological study was a rarity. The "silents," because of their technical limitations, were forced to deal with character depiction on a relatively superficial basis. Revelation of character had to be achieved almost entirely in visual terms; the villain was easily recognized as the guy who always kicked the defenseless dog, twisted his waxed moustache, or foreclosed on the widow. The hero, on the other hand, patted dogs on the head, helped old ladies across the street, and always shaved. Even though a look, a gesture, or a movement can provide subtle commentary on characterization, visual revelation of character is necessarily limited. Sound offered the film maker the means by which he could avoid clichés, and explore character in depth.

And yet despite the numerous possibilities that the addition of sound had opened up, the early sound films were pedestrian and disappointing. Film appeared to have regressed to the primitiveness of the first of the silent films. The reasons for this were both technical and economic.

Converting to sound was an expensive proposition which was further complicated by the fact that the sound film was developed prior to and during the depression. Understandably, there was some hesitancy on the part of the studios and theater owners to convert their facilities. Everyone wanted to be sure that the sound system would not only work properly, but that it would also prove popular with the public. As it turned out, those studios that resisted the transition met with economic disaster, for it was clear that the audiences demanded talking films. Although the finances were made available for the transition to sound by various moneyed interests, there was usually a string attached. The investors insisted on having one of their representatives sitting on the board of the motion picture studio. Thus, men who had no experience whatsoever in film were placed in policy-making positions.

Within a year (1928), the entire makeup of the film industry had undergone radical changes. Convinced that it was the spoken word that was attracting the larger audiences, Hollywood began a large scale recruiting program to bring in directors from Broadway, as well as playwrights and actors with theatrical backgrounds. Suddenly, many of the directors of the silent era found themselves out of work. Similarly, a number of popular actors and actresses of the silent screen became unemployable because of foreign accents, peculiar voice qualities, or awkward diction. At least temporarily, the distinctive cinematic qualities of film appeared lost; the early sound films had regressed to little more than "canned theater."

But the most crippling blow to the industry was traceable to the tyranny of the sound expert and his omnipresent microphone. In an earlier chapter, it was mentioned that one of the significant break-throughs in the development of film was the freeing of the camera from its fixed position. Sound changed all that, making the camera once again static and immobile. The early cameras were noisy pieces of machinery, their gears set up a din that was readily picked up by the microphones. To inhibit the noise, they were placed in a soundproof box, referred to as the "ice box" and, once again, the action was staged before the lens of a static camera.

In addition to the static camera, film was further shackled by the sound expert's microphone. It was the sound expert, rather than the director, who decided where the actors would be placed and which shots could be taken; artistic considerations were suddenly made sub-servient to the demands of sound. For a period of time, the result was a tiresome parade of incredibly static, stagey, talky motion pictures that were replete with every conceivable sound known to man. The artistry and subtlety of the best of the silent films appeared to be lost forever.

But, fortunately, the "canned theater" debacle didn't prevail for very long. A group of talented and creative directors such as Ernst Lubitsch, Reuben Mamoulian, Lewis Milestone and King Vidor began to discover the means by which they could circumvent the tyranny of sound.

Prior to technical innovations such as cameras that operated silently or the process of "blimping" (housing the camera in a soundproof box), the discovery—which critic Arthur Knight attributes to Ernst Lubitsch[5]—was made that a film did not have to be all talking, nor did the sound have to be recorded synchronously; the audio could be added later or "dubbed in." The breakthrough was significant: The camera could now be freed from the imprisonment of the soundproof box, it could be taken "off ice." That sound could be added later also implied that the techniques developed during the silent era were still valid; the camera could once again move unimpaired from long shot to close-up, and silent editing techniques were as viable as before. Dubbing also made it possible for the camera to extend its range. Previously, outdoor shots had been technical nightmares for sound technicians because there was a surfeit of sound that frequently drowned out the lines of the actors. The actors as well enjoyed new freedom, for they were not entirely limited by the hearing range of the microphones.

Not only was the director able to resume his rightful role in the film process, but he also discovered that he could bring sound, like the visual image, under his control. Prior to the post-synchronous recording of sound, nearly every sound on the set was transcribed verbatim. The extreme density of sound, noise and music had the effect of undermining the visuals of the film. But because the director was able to become more selective in his use of sound, the visuals could once again dominate the screen.

That the camera could be employed independently of sound suggested that sound could also be used independently of the image. Sound, it was learned, was not necessarily limited to just what was pictured. The early trend in sound films was to record visually everything that made a noise—the viewer hears a ringing and simultaneously sees a bell. But, in reality, there are many sounds that emanate from unseen sources: a plane flying overhead, a train in the distance, or a dog baying at the moon. Using sounds that lay outside the range of the camera not only extended the scope of the film experience but also made it possible for the director to establish a mood, suggest a place, or oppose an image with a contrary sound. Film makers began to examine the creative potentialities of sound. The adoption of the interior monologue was just one of these developments.

Soon after the introduction of sound, there followed a rash of theoretical proclamations concerning its proper use in film. Some of the more articulate theorists were the Russians, Sergei Eisenstein, V. I. Pudovkin, G. Alexandrov and the Frenchman, René Clair.

Understandably, Eisenstein, Pudovkin and Alexandrov viewed sound as a means of extending their theories of montage. In 1930, Eisenstein drew up a manifesto, which was signed by Pudovkin and Alexandrov. It read, in part:

> The success of Soviet films on the world's screen is due, to a significant degree, to those methods of montage which they first revealed and consolidated.

Therefore, for the further development of the cinema, the important moments will be only those that strengthen and broaden the montage methods of affecting the spectator.

ONLY A CONTRAPUNTAL USE of sound in relation to the visual montage piece will afford a new potentiality of montage development and perfection.

THE FIRST EXPERIMENTAL WORK WITH SOUND MUST BE DIRECTED ALONG THE LINE OF ITS DISTINCT NON-SYNCHRONIZATION WITH VISUAL IMAGES.[6]

Eisenstein felt that the real value of sound lay in its ability to create new cinematic forms, to orchestrate sound contrapuntally with the visual images, rather than merely record a credible illusion of reality. Pudovkin, on another occasion, pointed out that, in reality, sound rarely parallels the visual image we see. We don't, he observed, gaze at a speaker fixedly, but rather our eyes shift around, observing first one thing, then another; periodically, our eyes will return to the speaker.

Similarly, in France, René Clair was offering his own contributions to the theory of sound. Like the Russians, Clair felt that sound need not restrict itself to a faithful transcription of reality. Clair observed that the early "talkies," which recorded nearly every available sound, produced an artificial effect.[7] From this observation he concluded that a sound needed to be selected as carefully as an image: which particular sounds or sounds was to be determined by the demands of the scene. The ear, he felt, was as discriminating towards a sound as the eye was to an image. In a battle scene, for instance, the protagonist might very likely blot out the din of explosions and gunfire and only be conscious of the labored breathing of his wounded comrade. In his own films, Clair avoided sound that held only novelty interest and searched, instead, for the sounds that assisted the viewer to better understand the action.

In the late twenties and early thirties, developments in sound engineering were making it technically possible for film makers to employ sound more creatively. The noiseless camera was soon perfected and existing recording equipment became more sophisticated. However, there still remained the problem of developing a more positive means of synchronizing sound and image.

In their initial forays into sound, Warner Brothers had relied on wax disks for sound. Although the disks did provide the means to synchronize sound and image, they were far from satisfactory. Frequently, the sound would get out of "sync," causing the audio to lag behind or run ahead of the image. The first real breakthrough in synchronization came with the development of the optical sound track. With this method, the sound could now be scribed directly onto the film; this eliminated duplication of equipment, and ensured perfect synchronization.

In the optical sound process, the microphones record the sound, and the recorded sound is then translated into electrical impulses. These electrical impulses are "photographed" as visual patterns which are in turn scribed alongside the visual images. The projector "reads" these images by means of a scanning light, and the visual pattern is reconverted to the originally recorded sounds. The optical sound track remained in use throughout the 1940's. In the 1950's magnetic tape, which made immediate playback possible, superseded optical sound. Today, magnetic tape is still the most common method of recording and editing sound.

In today's cinema, the use of sound can be described in terms of four major areas: synchronous sound, asynchronous sound, silence, and music.

Synchronous sound (from the Greek word *sunkhronos: sun,* meaning same, and *khronos,* meaning time) is sound that occurs simultaneously with the image. The viewer, in this instance, sees a character speaking and concurrently hears what he is saying. Synchronous sound, as pointed out earlier, dominated the early sound films where the emphasis was on the novelty of sound and virtually everything that made a noise was pictured. Although synchronous sound is probably the least imaginative use of sound, it is at the same time, the most necessary and frequently employed type.

Asynchronous sound, on the other hand, is said to occur when the image and the sound track do not, in reality, occur simultaneously. To use Pudovkin's example again, the viewer hears the voice of the speaker but sees the face of the person to whom he is speaking. The uses to which asynchronous sound can be put are virtually unlimited. A character, in the course of conversation, might make mention of San Francisco and the viewer sees on the screen an image of a cable car or of the Golden Gate Bridge. On the screen there could appear an image of a woman screaming, but the spectator hears the shrill wail of a siren.

Or perhaps there is a shot of two small children fighting, but the sound track carries the cacaphony of the sounds of war.

There is an extremely interesting use of sound in Alain Resnais' *Hiroshima, Mon Amour* (1959). Below, in an excerpt from Part One of Marguerite Duras' scenario for the film, an unnamed French woman and a Japanese engineer or architect "discuss" Hiroshima.

He: You saw nothing in Hiroshima. Nothing.

(To be used as often as desired. A woman's voice, also flat, muffled, monotonous, the voice of someone reciting, replies:)

She: I saw everything. Everything.

(Fusco's music, which has faded before this initial exchange, resumes just long enough to accompany the woman's hand tightening on the shoulder again, then letting go, then caressing it. The mark of fingernails on the darker flesh. As if this scratch could give the illusion of being a punishment for: "No. You saw nothing in Hiroshima." Then the woman's voice begins again, still calm, colorless, incantatory:)

She: The hospital, for instance, I saw it. I'm sure I did. There is a hospital in Hiroshima. How could I help seeing it?

(The hospital, hallways, stairs, patients, the camera coldly objective. (We never see her seeing.) Then we come back to the hand gripping--and not letting go of--the darker shoulder.)

He: You did not see the hospital at Hiroshima. You saw nothing at Hiroshima.

(Then the woman's voice becomes--more impersonal. Shots of the museum. The same blinding light, the same ugly light here as at the hospital. Explanatory signs, pieces of evidence from the bombardment, scale models, mutilated iron, skin, burned hair, wax models, etc.)

```
She: Four times at the museum . . .

He: What museum in Hiroshima?

She: Four times at the museum in Hiroshima. I saw people
     walking around. The people walk around, lost in
     thought, among the photographs, the reconstructions,
     for want of something else, among the photographs, the
     photographs, the reconstructions, for want of
     something else, the explanations, for want of
     something else. . . .⁸
```

The conception and realization of this scene are brilliant. Dramatically portraying one of the most ghastly atrocities in the history of mankind without succumbing to either sentimentality or propaganda is no mean feat. Duras' scenario succeeds by means of a subtle use of asynchronous sound supported by carefully selected images.

The camera reveals that the man and the woman, both naked, are in bed. Nudity not only dramatizes the frailty and defenselessness of the couple, but also recalls the helplessness of the victims of Hiroshima. The flat, colorless voices preclude sentimentality and yet convincingly portray the devastating effect that the bombing of Hiroshima has had on the speakers' sensibilities. The incantatory repetition, readily apparent in the woman's last speech, underwrites the feeling of despair. The use of synchronous sound, in this instance, makes a significant contribution to our understanding of the visual images. The shots of the hospital and the museum are, of course, asynchronous to the dialogue. Although the man denies that the woman has seen anything, the reality of the shots of the hospital and museum are indelibly etched into the memory of the spectator. The woman's affirmation of what she has seen, followed by the man's denial, may appear perplexing, but the man's denial succinctly points up the impossibility of "talking about" Hiroshima.

The advantages of asynchronous sound are fairly apparent. Asynchronous sound can either provide additional support for an image, as in the case of a shot of the devastation of a bombed-out village accompanied by a forlorn scream, or counterpart an image, for instance, by showing an image of an empty football stadium, and recording the cheering of the crowds.

Asynchronous sound has also been employed in some films as a transitional device. In *Goodbye, Columbus* (1969), for example, the film's protagonist, Neil, is seen in conversation with his aunt. As this scene fades out and another showing Neil driving across town fades in, their conversation continues on the sound track. In addition to bridging the two scenes, this particular use of sound seems to suggest that the conversation remains in Neil's mind even though he has physically left his aunt behind him.

Silence is usually thought of as a negative value—the absence of sound—but, ironically, it was the sound film that made it possible for silence to attain positive value. Handled appropriately, silence can have significant dramatic impact on an audience. If silence precedes an action, it tends to highlight the moment, set it within a dramatic frame. In a courtroom, the man on trial stands to defend himself . . . the courtroom becomes hushed and attentive as it awaits his speech. A woman is sitting in a near-empty room, waiting for a man who she has reason to believe might kill her. The silence of her vigil will be heavily laden with tension for the audience. Silence can also be employed to impart a quality of strangeness, even of horror, to the familiar. A busy street corner, deprived of familiar noises, becomes, somehow, a threatening, alien landscape. As might be assumed from the previous examples, the use of silence in a film is frequently associated with tension, suspense and danger. Michelangelo Antonioni, for example, made use of huge "blocks" of silence in his highly acclaimed *Blowup* (1967).

The advent of the sound film created a more aurally sensitive audience as well. The quality of a sound became nearly as important as the rendering of an image. One significant change for the better was in the film use of dialogue. The "silent" films, for example, tended to employ a dialogue that was pompous, artificial and theatrical in nature. In the silent film, the subtitles represented an intrusive interruption of the film experience; consequently, the tendency was not only to keep the number of subtitles to a minimum but to convey only enough information to make the visuals understandable to the audience. When sound arrived, dialogue was no longer intrusive, but integral. However, dialogue, in the sound film, made quite different demands than the dialogue of the "silents," or even of the theater.

Language, in the theater, represents a significant portion of the play-going experience. The plays of Shakespeare, Marlowe, Sheridan, Yeats and Eliot are studied as frequently by students of literature as they are by students of drama. The reason is fairly obvious: Drama employs a highly literate language. But because of the inherent differences of the theatrical and film experience, the sound film required a substantially different language. Theater tends to employ more artifice than film; its audience accepts certain conventions—the removal of the fourth wall, stage whispers, soliloquies, scenery—as part of the theatrical experience. A rhetorical language is appropriate to theater art. But the conventions of cinema are not the same. Film tends to be more "realistic" than theater. Furthermore, because of the camera's ability to move within inches of a subject and portray the action from the vantage point of the protagonist, and even, in some instances, to delineate subjective states of consciousness, the film, in this sense, represents a more intimate genre. Consequently, the dialogue of film has to be lifelike: its language must closely approximate everyday speech. The film maker's art is also primarily a visual art—when meaning can be conveyed by an image, action or a gesture, dialogue becomes superfluous. Even the most cursory examination of the script of a play and a scenario for a film will reveal that the speeches in theater tend to be two to three times as long as equivalent speeches in film. (It will also be observed that the meaning of the play is discoverable within its language—clearly, this is not the case with film.) Thus, the representative dialogue of today's films tends to be terse, understated and, above all, realistic.

A classic case of the inimicality between literary dialogue and screen dialogue occurred in the much-publicized encounter between novelist F. Scott Fitzgerald and director Joseph L. Mankiewicz in the late '30's. Fitzgerald had written the dialogue for a film entitled *Three Comrades;* one of the film's actresses, Margaret Sullavan, complained that most of the lines were literally unspeakable, so Mankiewicz himself rewrote much of the dialogue. Fitzgerald was enraged and promptly wrote Mankiewicz.

> For nineteen years with two years out for sickness, I've written best-selling entertainment, and my dialogue is supposedly right up at top. But I've learned from the script that you've suddenly decided that it isn't good dialogue and you can take a few hours off and do much better.[9]

Mankiewicz argued, however, that the changes he made "cast . . . [no] more of a reflection on Fitzgerald's novels than the bad plays of Henry

James cast on his great novels"[10] Mankiewicz attempted to define the difference between writing a novel and writing for the screen:

> The novelist has an entirely different relationship with his reader than the screenwriter [or playwright] has with his audience. With a book, the relationship is between the printed page and the reader's intellect. The response is cerebral. On the screen [and the stage], the dialogue is heard, there is no time for cerebration—the response is to the rhythm and sound of the speech almost as much as to its content.[11]

The film maker, in addition to learning to cope with the written word, had to contend with other factors. He had to make sure, for example, that the dialogue matched the image. In the theater, nearly all dialogue originates from approximately the same position, the confines of the stage. But, in the film, actors are frequently widely separated spatially. The film maker needs to be sure that the voice of a character who is standing twenty-five feet from the camera sounds as though it were twenty-five feet away. The sound must be proportionate to the image. And, unlike the dramatist, who deals almost entirely with dialogue, the film maker must orchestrate incidental noise as well as music.

As was mentioned earlier, music had always represented a significant aspect of the film experience. When sound was introduced, the changes that music underwent were not so much quantitative as qualitative. The optical sound track, which ensured perfect synchronization of sound and image, raised the use of music in film to the status of a subtle art. Even in the days of the "silent" film, music had been successfully employed to suggest a mood or augment the drama of a particular scene, but now music could expand the reality of a shot as well as sustain dramatically important musical motifs. For example, if the camera pans the streets of Bombay as the audience listens to sitar music, the "atmosphere," or the feeling of being in Bombay is intensified. Again, if a young man is beaten nearly senseless by a group of hoodlums behind a dance hall, the recurrence of the song that the band was playing at the time of the beating has the effect of recalling the incident for the audience as well as for the young man.

Although music represents a more "unnatural" use of sound than dialogue or noise, it is susceptible to the principles of synchronous and asynchronous sound. Obviously, if the audience sees a trio of musicians playing and simultaneously hears jazz, the use of music is synchronous. Likewise, it might be argued that a shot of a riverboat making its way down the Mississippi accompanied by strains of "Old Man River" would also be synchronous, for the use of sound, in this instance, is predictably supportive and offers no additional information. However, if the screen represents two jet fighters engaged in a dogfight but the accompanying sound track plays a stately minuet, the effect is quite different. Notice that the visuals represent one thing—two planes engaged in aerial combat; the sound track another—seventeenth-century dance music—but the combination gives rise to a third element: a sardonically grim dance of death.

The above example represents a more imaginative use of sound than merely duplicating the image by recording the scream of jet engines and the rattle of machine-gun fire. Creative use of sound is usually characterized by the fact that the contribution of sound is either independent of or supportive to the image rather than duplicative.

It is possible, for example, for a film maker to replace a shot with a sound. If there is a critical scene in which the protagonist of the film, a woman, is being deserted by the man she loves, it is far more dramatically effective to hold the camera on her distressed face as the man walks out, slamming the door behind him, than to actually show the man's departure. The sound of the slammed door makes it unnecessary to show him leaving and, more importantly, the audience wants to see the woman's response.

Frequently, a film maker will alter a sound for dramatic emphasis. In a film about competitive amateur snow skiing called *Downhill Racer* (1970), there are several shots which show how a dangerous downhill run appears from the vantage point of the skier; the sole portion of him that is visible in the frame are the tips of his skis; the audience hears only his labored breathing. Obviously, in reality, other sounds would be present, but their omission and the stress on the racer's breathing, emphasize the arduousness of the run. Likewise, if the protagonist of a film is lost in the woods at night, exaggerating the cries of animals, the crackling of twigs, and the sound of the wind in the trees is not only dramatically effective but psychologically legitimate, for it appproximates the way in which the character would respond to these vaguely threatening noises.

Synthetic sound, which represents electronically produced noises that have no counterpart in reality, is another important source of creative sound. Here, sound is attained in unorthodox ways: by running tapes backward, by mixing and overlaying sounds from disparate sources, by recording the noises of various pieces of electronic equipment and orchestrating them into musical motifs. Thus far, the use of synthetic sound has been restricted to relatively limited areas: science fiction and the aural depiction of altered or abnormal states of consciousness and fantasy. But it is obvious that the presence of electronic sound in our everyday lives is increasing daily. It can be predicted with some surety that synthetic sound and electronic music will widen their sphere of influence in the coming years.

Inasmuch as sound, on film, is represented by optical patterns, some film makers have undertaken experiments of directly scribing the sound onto the film without benefit of recording equipment. One of the pioneers in this area is the Canadian film maker, Norman McLaren. McLaren, who employs this technique in two of his award-winning short subjects, *Dots* and *Loops,* created a whole new range of sound possibilities with this method. Although his technique offers obviously unique potentialities in the film maker, it would appear that the limited applicability of this method, compounded by the considerable investment of time required to hand scribe the sound track, would necessarily limit widespread usage.

Even though it is difficult to draw up any dogmatic rules governing the function of sound in film, it is possible to indicate what comprises ineffective usage. Symbolic use of sound, for instance, should be comprehensible to a reasonably perceptive member of the audience. For example, if a film maker portrays a couple having a marvelous time riding a cable car in San Francisco, but attempts to foreshadow the forthcoming end of this gaiety by means of a mournful wail of a siren faintly heard in the background, the chances are that the effect will be completely lost on the audience. The viewer, responding to the couple's gaiety, will perceive the noise of the siren as just one more of many similar sounds that comprise the total gestalt of the sounds of the city. On the other hand, the film maker might show the same couple seated in an outdoor restaurant quietly talking, and have the woman say, "I can't remember being happier. I keep telling myself that it can't last," and there follows a quiet moment as the couple looks at each other. In the interim of silence, the wail of the siren is discernible in the background. In this instance, the use of the siren would be clear: happiness is transitory. Preceded by her speech, the distant siren strikes an ominous note.

Even though asynchronous sound represents one of the more creative uses of sound, the juxtaposition of sound and image must be carefully considered by the film maker so as not to confuse the audience. If the film maker shows the audience shots of commuters being herded into subway trains by conductors and simultaneously plays the sounds of lowing cattle, the juxtaposition of sound and image is comprehensible. On the other hand, the audience may witness a scene in which a young man is being taunted and ridiculed by his elders; he stalks from the room slamming the door behind him, but rather than hearing the slam of a door, the audience hears the sharp report of a pistol shot. Later in the film, the audience learns that the young man has gravitated to a life of crime. The sound of the pistol shot is an attempt to relate the young man's humiliation to his life of crime, but the audience's response to the sound of the pistol shot will probably be one of confusion. The suggested relationship between the scene and pistol shot, tenuous at best, requires either further elaboration or total elimination.

Even from this brief discussion of sound, it should be clear that creative and effective use of sound departs from the sound we contend with in everyday life. Sound, in film, is characterized by selectivity and restraint, qualities which are rarely present in everyday reality, for we are subject to a constant bombardment of random, and usually meaningless noises—the whine of tires against pavement, the labored drone of a truck engine, the periodic shriek of a siren, the whisper of a jet passing overhead, voices, radios, television, birds, machines, wind, rain . . . But the fact that the film maker chooses to ignore these extraneous noises is not an arbitrary decision: When involved in a situation, we, too, choose to differentiate between the superfluous and the significant. As the gestalt psychologists would describe it, we select from the total configuration of experience a figure that commands our attention. Everything else recedes to the status of the less important background. Effective use of sound, then, represents a departure from or variation on reality.

The skillful application of sound can also be evaluated by the kind of contribution it makes to the image. Does the sound merely duplicate the image, explaining to the audience aurally what has already been understood visually, or does the sound increase perception of meaning? Can it, for example, supplement the image's significance? Imagine a camera panning a section of a polluted stream objectively recording man's senseless contamination of his environment; the audience hears only the anguished wail of a small child—the recipient of this dubious heritage. The cry of the child might supplement the audience's understanding of the image. Or perhaps the audience witnesses a small crowd encouraging two young boys to fight. The sounds of shouting from the crowd give way to the sounds of war. In this instance, the meaning of the image has been further extended by the sound track: The juxtaposition of sound and image seems to suggest that society, represented by the crowd surrounding the two boys, encourages violence and that war represents the logical culmination of a culture's approbation of it.

The sound film, now over forty years old, is still undergoing change. Electronic sound and music as well as hand-scribed sound tracks are subjects of constant experimentation by underground and university film makers. Stereophonic sound, which is now employed in all Cinerama productions as well as many conventional films, augments an audience's experience of "being there" through the use of multiple sound tracks and speakers. Michael Wadleigh's documentary/celebration *Woodstock* (1970), for example, represents an outstanding example of the contemporary film's ability, through multiple sound tracks, to create the illusion of sound in depth. The sophisticated recording and playback equipment of the larger studios make it very probable that future audiences will experience total sound environments as part of the film experience. Multiple-track recording channelled through speakers placed throughout an auditorium could reproduce the complex sound spectrum of a modern city or the subtle interplay of sounds that occur when a sailboat tacks across a bay. Although a total sound environment could represent an exciting film experience for an audience, it could also retrogress to mere novelty interest. Any technical innovation should ultimately be subservient to an artist's creativity and vision. When technique serves only its own ends, the art of the film suffers.

REFERENCES

1. Kracauer, Siegfried, *Theory of Film* (Oxford University Press, New York, 1960), p. 134.

2. For a more detailed account of the emergence and subsequent development of the sound film, see Arthur Knight's *The Liveliest Art* (New American Library, New York, 1957).

3. Kracauer, p. 133.

4. Stephenson, Ralph and Debrix, J. R., *The Cinema as Art* (Penguin Books, Baltimore, 1965), p. 183.

5. Knight, Arthur, *The Liveliest Art* (New American Library, New York, 1957), p. 151.

6. Eisenstein, Sergei, *Film Form* and *The Film Sense* (Meridan, Cleveland, 1957), *Film Form* pp. 257–258.

7. MacCann, Richard Dyer (ed.), *Film: A Montage of Theories* (Dutton, New York, 1966), p. 39.

8. Duras, Marguerite and Resnais, Alain, *Hiroshima, Mon Amour* (Evergreen, New York, 1961), pp. 15–17.

9. Sarris, Andrew, "Mankiewicz of The Movies," *Show*, March, 1970, p. 29.

10. *Ibid.,* p. 29.

11. *Ibid.,* p. 29.

In Hiroshi Teshigahara's *Woman in the Dunes* (1964), the ever-present sand becomes virtually one of the principal characters.

FIGURATIVE LANGUAGE:

FILM AND LITERATURE

Nothing can resist the unifying power of the metaphor; anything conceivable by the human mind can be compared to something else.

PIER PAOLO PASOLINI[1]

John Cassavetes' *Faces,*
(1968), discussed
in Chapter Two, brutally
depicts the frustration
and not-so-quiet despair
of a middle-class
American couple at the
mid-century.

Courtesy of Walter Reade 16,
241 East 34th Street
New York City, N.Y. 10016

"All Animals Are Equal
But Some Animals
Are More Equal Than
Others" says
comrade pig in the 1955
feature-length cartoon
of George Orwell's
allegory, *Animal Farm.*

Courtesy of Contemporary
Films/McGraw-Hill

Quite often in a film a landscape becomes freighted with symbolic meaning. Here is a shot from Michelangelo Antonioni's 1960 *L'Avventura.*

Courtesy of Janus Films, Inc.

In Federico Fellini's 1959 study of modern-day Roman decadence, *La Dolce Vita,* the characters come face-to-face with a real monster from the depths.

Courtesy of Audio Film Center/
Ideal Pictures

N THE preceding chapters, the considerations of meaning in film were, for the most part, allied with the artist's use of technique. It was pointed out, for example, that a film maker consciously selects a particular lens for a shot because he knows beforehand that its properties will cause an image to be presented in a particular way: A telephoto lens used on a crowd, for instance, will emphasize the crowd's density. This could, in turn, depending on the film's theme, stress the crowded conditions of contemporary living in an over-populated world. But the question of meaning, of course, is not something that is reducible to technique alone—meaning is intimately related to the artist's vision, his way of seeing the world, his sense of moral or aesthetic values, his capacity to respond emotionally to situations, and his sensitivity to the nuances of language, whether it be the language of literature or the language of film.

A sensitive writer is conscious of the fact that most words are doubly weighted with meaning. On the more obvious level, they carry a denotative, or dictionary meaning; on another level, they bear a connotative meaning which refers to a word's suggestive or associational implications. For example, if a writer is attempting to describe a character who is lean or slender of figure, any one of the following words would accomplish that task: "thin," "petite," or "scrawny." Each of the three words has approximately the same denotative meaning; however, the connotations of these words differ considerably. The word "thin," for example, is a relatively neutral word that simply describes the individual's build. "Petite," on the other hand, moves in the direction of an implied judgment: it carries the positive connotations of a delicate and fragile beauty. "Scrawny," however, implies a negative judgment—the image of a gaunt, bony, somewhat disheveled figure comes to mind. Which of these three possibilities the writer will ultimately decide upon will depend on how he wants the reader to perceive this particular character—neutrally, positively or negatively.

Everyone, in the course of a day, will, at one point or another, consciously or unconsciously, weigh the connotations of a word before uttering it. Thus, it is relatively common practice to distinguish between a word's denotation and its connotation. Rarely, however, is an image considered in terms of denotation and connotation, and yet it is clear that an image is subject to much the same criteria as a word.

In the previous example, the denotative value of the three words was approximately the same, but their connotations were quite different. Let us consider an image whose denotation will remain unaffected even though its connotations are altered. Imagine a wooden, two-storied Victorian house that was built just after the turn of the century on a steep hill in San Francisco. The building's straight, somewhat severe lines are broken up by beautiful and ornate woodwork that adorns the corners and eaves of the house. The house itself is painted avocado green and the trim is done in black. A huge, hand-carved wooden door with a leaded glass window dominates the front of the house. It looks as though it has about a dozen rooms. This brief, somewhat sketchy description would represent the quantitative, or denotative meaning, of an image of a house.

Assume that a film maker wishes to film three different takes of this same house, but he wants to alter the connotations in each take. For the first take, he might set up his camera across the street from the house. In the flat, colorless light of the noonday sun, he films the house as a passerby might see it. The resulting image is relatively neutral: The house appears to be a well-preserved architectural remnant of the past. The following day, at sunrise, the film maker records his second take of the house. This time he angles the camera in such a way as to emphasize the rich ornamental woodwork, and the jewel-like quality of the leaded glass window. The gold of the red-orange sun spills over the roof and sides of the house, framing it in a rich play of color. In this instance, the house acquires an air of nostalgia: The image calls up associations of a less harried, more genteel life style, an existence that was, in many ways, less complicated and demanding than that of today's world. Later that same day, in the early hours of the evening, the film maker records his third and final take. This time, he moves the camera very close to the house and positions it so that it points upward at an unusual angle. In this take, the house appears very different. The unusual and low camera angle causes the viewer to look up at the house, which now seems overpowering and somehow intimidating. Since it is early in the evening, large areas of the house are in shadows; this also contributes to the feeling of mystery and eeriness. The house might be huge—"Gothic" mansion, perhaps the scene of clandestine, mysterious, or evil rites.

In each of the three takes, the denotative, or literal meaning of the image—a two-storied Victorian house—remains unchanged, but the connotations of the image are altered. The first portrays the house neutrally; the second romanticizes it; whereas the third renders the house as mysterious and forbidding. The first take would easily lend itself to a documentary on San Francisco; the second, perhaps a shot from a musical or a comedy; the third, a story of horror or intrigue. By manipulating the *connotations* of the image, the film maker is not only able to convey more information within a given image, but he is also able to alter the emotional overtones of the image itself.

In literature, connotation forms the basis of figurative language and literary tropes. Figurative language, which includes the metaphor, the simile, personification, paradox, hyperbole and understatement, is a tremendously important aspect of the literary experience, for it provides the writer with the means to communicate far more than he ever could if he adhered exclusively to a literal use of language. Figurative language is a departure from the conventional and ordinary uses of language. By employing it, the writer is able to coin a fresh or unique expression or perhaps even startle his reader into considering a subject in a new or unusual light.

Figures of speech, or literary tropes, are nonliteral uses of language. Robert Frost once said that "Poetry provides the one permissible way of saying one thing and meaning another." Frost's statement points up an important aspect of figurative language, namely, that it is able to say one thing in terms of something else. For example, if a person says, "It grows dark slowly at sundown," then he uses language in a conventional and informative sense. However, if the same speaker said, "The evening approaches on padded cat's feet," he would be using language in a figurative sense: The image of evening as a cat brings to mind those qualities of a cat that are equally applicable to sundown—languor, softness, perhaps stealthiness in the sense of a gradual change from light to dark. By using language figuratively, the speaker was not only able to communicate more to his listener but he was able to do it more vividly.

Connotation, it has been argued, is the basis of figurative language. If an image can be affected by connotation, and it appears as though it can, then it would be useful to consider if there is such a thing as a figurative use of an image and whether there are equivalents in film for the metaphor, the simile and other related literary tropes.

In its broadest sense, a figurative image may be said to occur whenever a film maker, for the sake of emphasis or freshness, departs from the conventional way of filming a subject. For example, if the film maker's subject is a group of wealthy women who are all attired in expensive clothes and elaborately plumed hats, the conventional way of filming them would probably be via an eye-level shot. But instead of filming the women in this manner, the film maker positions his camera so that it is directly above the women, pointed down on their hats. Thus, the viewer observes only the feathered plumage and the tops of their hats: This particular shot would have the effect of portraying the women as rare and exotic bird-like creatures. Or perhaps a young man is hugging a close and trusted female acquaintance while he joyously tells her that he has fallen in love with a girl whom both of them know. Rather than showing the couple in a predictable embrace, the film maker decides to show the young man behind the woman with his arms about her waist and his chin resting on the top of her head. In a close-up, the audience sees the lower part of the young man's face and the upper part of the girl's face: The young man wears a beaming smile whereas the girl's eyes are brimming with tears. Instantly the audience realizes, as the young man does not, that the girl being embraced has been in love with the young man for some time. Both of these shots could be considered examples of the figurative use of a camera: in both instances, the images are unorthodox and striking, and both convey more meaning than conventional shot.

In literary works, a very common figure of speech is the metaphor. Basically, the metaphor is an implied comparison between two things which are essentially unlike: i.e., "My love is a red rose." Unlike an ordinary comparison, in which there is usually no departure from the conventional denotations of words (i.e., "A car is faster than a horse"), the metaphor represents a richer, denser kind of comparison which, on a superficial level, appears to be illogical. How, for example, is a woman a rose? Obviously the speaker does not mean to imply the woman is underweight (stem-like body) and has an oversized head (the bloom), but wants to suggest a beauty that is delicate, soft, perhaps sweetly scented. When Jaques, a character in Shakespeare's *As You Like It,* says: "All the world's a stage/And all the men and women merely players. . . ." (II. vii. 739–40) he states that the world is a gigantic stage and then suggests by means of a metaphor that the drama of life is enacted on it. By comparing individuals to players, Jaques reminds the audience that, like actors, people have entrances and exits (births and deaths) and that, in the course of their lifetimes, men are apt to play many different roles: infant, schoolboy, lover, soldier, justice, mature man, senile old man. . . .

Jaques' metaphor is expansive; that is, it takes the entire world as the basis of its comparison. Poet William Blake operates on an equally suggestive, but greatly reduced basis, when he says, "To see a world in a grain of sand. . . ." At first Blake's comparison appears to be illogical: a grain of sand is very minute, so how could it possibly be compared to a world? But when the two are considered at greater length, it becomes clear that there are some very suggestive analogies: In the immensity of the universe, the earth is of little more size or importance than a grain of sand; the shape of a grain of sand is like a miniature model of the world; a grain of sand is common and ordinary and yet unique because there is no other exactly like it, whereas the earth must be like other planets of the universe, and yet, it too is unique.

In literature, the metaphor forces the reader to consider the similarities of two apparently dissimilar things. Frequently, the metaphor has the effect of helping the reader to make fresh, unusual or unthought-of discoveries for himself. Film, of course, has its own equivalent for the metaphor, but there are some basic distinctions that separate the cinematic and the literary metaphor.

In order to create the film metaphor, the film maker juxtaposes two concrete images in such a way as to imply that one thing is the other. To use a simple example, a film maker sets up a camera in front of a grammar school; he shows the children waiting nervously and impatiently for the eight o'clock bell to sound. When the bell rings he shows some of the children flowing into the corridors of the school. This footage would imply one meaning. The film maker then goes to the local stockyard and, this time, he films a flock of sheep lined up awaiting entry to a slaughterhouse. This strip of film would imply yet another meaning. However, if the film maker splices these two strips of film together, creating a film metaphor, he forces his audience to consider how the two shots are similar. The basic metaphor is that the children are sheep. The audience notes that both the children and the sheep are herded about; that both are being prepared for a market; that their lives are subject to many pressures and influences over which they have no control; that they have no freedom. In this instance, the film meta-phor was created by dynamically opposing two different images. There are, however, other ways by which a film metaphor can be created.

John Howard Lawson, in his provocative study of audio-visual lan-guage and structure, *Film: The Creative Process,* gives an example of a film metaphor that was created by juxtaposing a seemingly unrelated sound track with a shot of a book:

> In *Handwriting,* a nine-minute film by Charles Rittenhouse, the spoken text is a poem:
>
> > Once I heard a white bird,
> > I studied its speckled wings,
> > I deciphered its markings.
>
> On the screen, the poet is turning the pages of a book, and the pages are compared to the bird's wings, the print to its speckled markings. If the words were accompanied by shots of the white bird, the images might be beautiful, but their relationship to the words would be pedestrian and unnecessary: something new is created by the juxtaposition of the bird and the book.[2]

As Lawson suggests, Rittenhouse's metaphoric comparison possesses a quality of freshness and unpredictability. Initially, the viewer would probably be perplexed by the seemingly unrelated combination of the bird and the book, but almost immediately he is sure to have the "ah hah" experience of recognizing how the two are alike. From that point on, he is able to derive both satisfaction and enjoyment in considering the correspondences shared by the bird and the book.

What most audiences would have been anticipating when they heard the line "Once I heard a white bird," is probably a shot of a seagull skimming over the tops of the waves. The predictability of this mundane association of word and image, however, would have had the effect of transforming the combination into a sort of audio-visual cliché—i.e., the "poetic" moment.

There are, of course, film clichés just as there are literary clichés. A cliché, in literature, is an expression or phrase that has simply become blunted or worn out through excessive usage: "green as grass," "a sickening thud," or "a clinging vine" are some obvious examples. Like-wise, if a film maker manages to employ a shot or a film comparison that is in any way suggestive, there is sure to be a raft of imitators. For instance, at one point in the history of film, the sex act was portrayed on the screen by means of exploding fireworks, waves crashing over rocks, or flames leaping up in a fireplace. Similarly, passages of time would be handled by showing pages being blown off calendars, the hands of a clock spinning around, or verdant landscapes dissolving into "winter wonderlands." Today's films have spawned a whole new crop of clichés: the obligatory pot party; the couple in bed together naked from the shoulders upward; couples in love running in slow motion across parks, along the water's edge, or through meadows; violence in slow motion. . . . The film cliché, predictably, is an excellent index of an enfeebled imagination.

When the writer or the film maker use the metaphor, the comparison between two things is implied. However, when a simile is used, the comparison is expressed. In the previously cited example of a metaphor from *As You Like It,* Jaques' line read, "All the world's a stage." If that same line were altered to read, "All the world is like a stage" then the line would become a *simile,* for the comparison would be expressed by the word "like." Nearly every literary simile makes use of some connective word such as "like," "as," "than," or "resembles."

However, it is much more difficult to distinguish the film metaphor from the film simile for, in film, there is no real equivalent for a connective word. Nevertheless, it could be argued that the two can be distinguished from each other on the basis of emphasis. In literature, for example, the simile is less emphatic than a metaphor: "he is like a pig," as opposed to "he is a pig." Similarly, the film simile is less forceful than the film metaphor. For example, a camera might show an expensively dressed woman pacing back and forth in a chic apartment; the next shot shows a well-groomed Persian cat pacing back and forth in another part of the same room; the third shot cuts back to the woman again. The juxtaposition of these shots creates a film simile. Allying the cat with the woman does not connote that they are the same, it merely implies that they are similar in some respects.

It is also possible for a film simile to occur within a single shot. A recent television commercial showed several owners grooming their dogs for a competition. What became readily apparent to the audience was the striking resemblances between the owners and their dogs: A heavy-set individual with large jowls was pictured grooming his bulldog and, next to him, a lean, delicate-looking greyhound was being positioned by a tall, thin, aesthetic-looking man. The simile, in film, provides the artist with a means to comment obliquely upon a character or a situation; the simile can obviously also help a viewer discover an important aspect of a character that may have easily gone unnoticed.

Another, somewhat allied figure of speech that is sometimes adopted by the film maker is personification. In poetry as well as prose, personification occurs when an abstraction, an inanimate object or something in nature, is endowed with human characteristics. "Death sings a mournful tune," would be an example of an abstraction personified; "the highway calls the traveller" an instance of an inanimate object which had been personified; "the tree spread its arms out against the sky" would represent an example of nature personified. When the artist uses personification, he demands that his audience identify the object or idea with a human being or at least a human characteristic. The frequency of personification in films is rare, but it does occur. The following four shots were taken from the screenplay of David Lean's film version of Charles Dickens' *Great Expectations* (1946):

4. MEDIUM CLOSE SHOT. Pip (a young boy) kneeling near tombstone. Wind gets louder. Pip looks around nervously towards the camera.

5. LONG SHOT. From Pip's eyeline of the leafless branches of a tree, which look to Pip like bony hands clutching at him.

6. MEDIUM CLOSE SHOT. Pip looks around as in #4.

7. MEDIUM SHOT. Of the trunk of an old tree from Pip's eyeline . . . The tree looks sinister to Pip like a distorted human body.[3]

In this particular scene, Lean's problem was to discover concrete correlatives for Pip's apprehension: this is accomplished by personifying the branches as bony hands and the old tree as a distorted human body. Ordinarily, the branches and trunk of the tree would simply represent part of the context of a scene but, by personifying them, they make a positive contribution to the scene. More obvious examples of personification appear in cartoons and animated films: Animals assume the characteristics of human beings; waves reach out, clutching at a foundering boat; trains and cars are endowed with personalities. The usefulness of personification, for the writer as well as the film maker, is its ability to suggest striking and unusual parallels between the human and the non-human.

An even more suggestive associational device, however, is the symbol. In Greek, the word *sumbolon* "means token for identification"; in Latin, *symbolum* means "sign" or "token." A sign or a token is, in a sense, a kind of shorthand device: On the highway, a diamond-shaped sign indicates to a driver that he should reduce his speed; in mathematics, the sign $+$ indicates that two quantities are to be added together. Through continued use, both of these particular signs have come to have a fairly explicit meaning. A symbol, like the sign or the token, also stands for something else, but it differs from both of these in that it is not only infinitely more potent, but much more richly suggestive. The sign does not arouse emotions, but the symbol can; conventional symbols, which are symbols whose meanings are relatively fixed through agreement, are frequently the objects of heated and passionate emotions: the Stars & Stripes, the cross, the six-pointed star of Judaism would represent some obvious examples. Frequently in literature, a particular word may be employed so consistently over a period of time that it attains the status of a conventional symbol. This has happened with many words; the rose, for example, has become synonymous with love, the snake with evil, and the nightingale with melancholy.

More frequently, however, the symbol does not have a fixed or generally agreed upon meaning but is as multi-faceted as a gem stone. Typically, the symbol is something that is concrete, i.e., it can be seen, smelled, heard or touched. It is possible for a symbol to be an object, such as the red letter "A" that Hester Prynne wears on her blouse in Hawthorne's *The Scarlet Letter;* a symbol could also be a whale as in Melville's *Moby Dick,* or perhaps a person such as the anxious Joseph K. in Franz Kafka's *The Trial.* Had Kafka given Joseph a full name, his symbolic value would have been diminished as a last name sets a person apart from his fellowmen. In the work, then, the artist usually gives the symbol unusual stress or emphasis; often this is accomplished through the use of repetition. Most symbols, however, are characterized by a quality of suggestive richness, a density, an air of mystery, and are not reducible to a single meaning.

In a film, the symbol functions precisely the same way as it does in a literary work; it is concrete, often slightly mysterious, and highly suggestive. As in literature, symbols in film derive their meanings from the total context of the work. Orson Welles' highly acclaimed *Citizen Kane,* for example, makes extensive use of symbolism. One of the opening shots of the film shows the decayed elegance of Kane's immense estate, Xanadu. In the course of the film, the audience learns that Kane has spent much of his lifetime building and furnishing this contemporary palace—thus, Xanadu becomes a symbol for his ponderous yet empty "success." The snowflake paperweight and the old sled, "Rosebud," in the same film, come to symbolize the normal childhood that Kane was never able to participate in; the acres of *objets d'art* that Kane surrounded himself with are symbolic of the beauty that was so conspicuously absent in his own life.

In many instances, it may require a period of time for a symbol to emerge. The authors of *The Motion Picture and the Teaching of English* point out how a physical landscape, over a period of time, can attain symbolic meaning:

> In Michelangelo Antonioni's *L'Avventura* (1960), the symbol of human alienation and loneliness comes not through a verbal image but through the whole first twenty-five minutes of pictures of people individually, or in pairs, picking their way along the jagged face of a great rock island in the Mediterranean, losing sight of each other, moving apparently aimlessly in what is a search for a girl who has disappeared from them, perhaps into the sea. The rocky surface, washed by a sea, is sharp as death and lovely as life—at one moment breathtaking in beauty and the next chilling in ferocity as it lashes the inlets where there is no chance for boat or man to come ashore safely.[4]

Quite often in a film, a landscape does acquire symbolic meaning: in Hiroshi Teshigahara's *Woman in the Dunes* (1964), the ever-present, constantly shifting sand almost attains the status of a mute, yet extremely expressive character. Roman Polanski's *Cul-de-Sac* (1966) takes place in a castle that is separated from the shore by a slender causeway; surrounded by the sea, the castle is both a trap for its occupants and a perverse world in miniature. And anyone who has seen the harsh Scandinavian landscapes of Ingmar Bergman's films will find it very difficult not to view Bergman's extremely suggestive settings in symbolic terms.

Frequently, a character in a film will emerge as a symbol. The symbolic character in film, as in literature, is usually ambiguously defined, his personality and characteristics tend to be emblematic or representative rather than highly individualized. In Federico Fellini's study of middle and upper-class dissolution, *La Dolce Vita* (1959), there are two instances in which a very simple young country girl appears. Next to nothing is known about her, but in contrast to the other characters in the film, who are either jaded, depraved or both, the girl stands out as a symbol of innocence, honesty and compassion. Sometimes a film maker will portray a character as a conventional symbol. In Ingmar Bergman's *The Seventh Seal* (1957), a stern, emaciated figure dressed in a black robe and cowl is the major antagonist of the film: No one is surprised when he tells the film's protagonist, a knight named Antonious Block, that he is called Death.

The film symbol, like the literary symbol, can be relatively simple or extremely complicated, depending on the kind and quantity of meaning that the artist has invested in it. What is clear, however, is the fact that the symbol demands from an audience an active participation both in it and the events which bring it into being. Ultimately, a member of the audience must determine for himself how a symbol is being used and what it represents.

A much simpler form of symbolism is allegory. The allegorical narrative tells a story beneath which there is yet another story. Most frequently, it will be found that the characters and events of the surface story correspond, usually in a one-to-one relationship, with characters and events of another time and place.

During the middle ages, the allegory, as a form, flourished: *Piers Plowman, The Pearl* and *The Nun's Priest's Tale* are just a few examples of medieval allegorical narratives that have been preserved. Today, the occurrence of the allegory is much less frequent. One famous example of a contemporary allegory, however, is George Orwell's *Animal Farm*. Orwell's terse novel is an excellent example of the allegorist "speaking in other terms": superficially, Orwell appears to be telling a tale about a barnyard insurgency, whereas he is actually writing a scathing indictment of the totalitarian state. As a result of the novella's popularity, *Animal Farm* was brought to the screen as a feature-length cartoon in 1955. More recently, John Barth has written a sprawling

Rabelaisian novel entitled *Giles Goat Boy.* In the novel, the world is presented as a gigantic university which has been divided into east campus and west campus. The parallels between the conditions of the contemporary world and Barth's university, between famous historical personages and the characters who populate the novel are too striking to be overlooked.

The recent French film *Z* (1969), directed by Costa-Gavras, utilizes many of the techniques of allegory. The story line is relatively simple: A pacifist leader comes to a certain unnamed European country to speak; during his stay, he is assassinated, and a subsequent inquiry reveals that the assassination was both encouraged, promoted and defended by military leaders of the unnamed state. Even though no particular country or individual is ever named, it is extremely difficult to ignore the obvious parallels of the events in *Z* to similar political situations in Greece, Spain, Czechoslovakia, Vietnam and the United States.

In its most simple form, allegory is the representation of something by something else. For example, in John Bunyan's famous allegory *The Pilgrim's Progress,* a man named Christian journeys towards a place called the Celestial City and along the way encounters characters such as Mr. Worldly Wiseman and the Giant Despair. In creating his Christian allegory, Bunyan renders concrete (Despair, Doubt, Promise, etc.) what is usually abstract. Likewise, in his dark, sardonic farce *Dr. Strangelove,* director Stanley Kubrick gives his characters such unlikely names as General Jack D. Ripper, Colonel Bat Guano, Captain Mandrake, Chief of Staff "Buck" Turgidson and President Merkin Muffley. (To say nothing of the ex-Nazi, Doktor Wierdeliebe, who, after the fall of the Reich, has become a prominent American scientist now called Dr. Strangelove.) In both the literary and the film allegory, characters' names are frequently obvious indications of what the characters are meant to represent. There are, of course, exceptions: William Golding's *Lord of the Flies* (brought to the screen in 1963 by Peter Brook) is an allegorical novel that does not use the names of the characters in an obvious fashion.

When the writer or the film maker utilizes allegory as a form, there is typically a discrepancy between what he appears to be saying and what he is actually saying. Much the same thing occurs when the artist, for the sake of freshness or emphasis, decides to make use of overstatement (sometimes referred to as hyperbole) or understatement.

For the artist, overstatement has a variety of uses: it can produce a comic effect, a serious emphasis, or it may merely be dramatically convincing, perhaps wildly fanciful. When Tennyson, in his poem *The Eagle,* describes the bird as being "close to the sun in lonely lands," he is making obvious use of overstatement, or hyperbole, for the reader knows that the earth is actually some 93,000,000 miles from the sun. Yet the line is persuasive; it portrays the eagle as a tremendously powerful figure that, from an immense height seems to lord over the vast territory that lies beneath him. The reader accepts the exaggeration because it manages to get at those qualities that people of all nations and times have admired in the eagle. Similarly, much of the comedy of America's earlier films was heavily dependent on the use of hyperbole or exaggeration. In Edward Cline's *Never Give a Sucker an Even Break* (1941), the laconic W. C. Fields offers to drive a woman, whom he believes is about to have a baby, to the local hospital. Fields speeds through the city narrowly averting disaster at every street corner. Terrified at his driving, the woman passes out; Fields, believing that she is about to give birth, drives even faster. The subsequent trip to the hospital is madness itself: cars careen around corners at incredible speeds, pedestrians are nearly run over, there are a half dozen minor collisions en route but, incredibly, no one is hurt.

The opposite of hyperbole, of course, is understatement. In understatement, there is a certain outrageousness because of the discrepancy between what the speaker is saying and his manner of saying it. Jonathan Swift, a master of understatement, once said, "Last week I saw a woman flayed, and you will hardly believe how much it altered her person for the worst." In *A Modest Proposal,* probably his best known example of understatement, Swift assigns himself the role of a "reasonable" and dedicated citizen who is addressing himself to the problem of Irish overpopulation. By means of a perfectly logical argument, he proposes a method by which the "excess" infants of Ireland could be made "useful members of the commonwealth"; he argues that the majority of the infants should be slaughtered at an early age and served up as a national dish, the remainder could be shipped abroad as a delicacy thus favorably augmenting the national treasury's balance of payments. Through understatement, Swift is arguing that "the English are devouring the Irish." Needless to say, he makes his point.

Film, of course, can readily utilize understatement in dialogue, but such a use of understatement would represent a literary rather than a cinematic trope. Understatement in film is either based upon a visual or aural discrepancy between what the audience is seeing and what they are being told, or by underplaying the audience's visual expectations.

Perhaps the audience is watching a mock documentary on "Man's Progress": The narrator waxes eloquent over man's engineering triumphs and the audience witness brief shots of suspension bridges, gigantic dams and an orbiting spaceship; the narrator then points out that man has made great strides in the field of medicine, and the screen shows some shots of an artificial limb, an X-ray machine and a heart transplant operation. The narrator goes on to enumerate man's contributions to civilization, but at one point he intones, "Man's progress, of course, necessitates some small sacrifices," and the viewer sees entire cities shrouded in smog, beaches littered with broken bottles, beer cans and papers, polluted streams and rivers, and thousands of cars jamming the arteries of a modern expressway. In relation to the appalling visuals, the audio represents a blatant example of understatement.

Although visual understatement can be utilized in many ways, it is most frequently made use of in comedy. A character standing on the edge of a bridge announces to the world that he cannot swim and is going to take his own life. He leaps from the bridge, but lands in ankle-deep water. A would-be saboteur vows to blow up a building, but when he depresses the plunger of the detonator only a whiff of smoke and a barely audible explosion takes place. Understatement frequently relies upon a reversal of expectations; consequently, it is similar in nature to irony.

In literature, as in film, irony can take several forms: verbal irony, dramatic irony, and irony of fate. All ironies depend upon an incongruity of some sort; usually either a discrepancy between what is said and what is intended or a discrepancy between what is expected and what actually happens.

Of the three ironies mentioned above, verbal irony is the closest to understatement; in fact, in many instances, it is very difficult to tell them apart. Verbal irony possesses a double-edged quality, it cuts two ways simultaneously. When Samuel Butler wrote, "I would not be—not quite —so pure as you," it appeared as though he were paying a compliment to the person he addressed, whereas he was actually doing just the opposite. In film, verbal irony is not entirely limited to dialogue: Wind and rain lashing a billboard that announces "Welcome to Florida, the Sunshine State" would be an obvious use of it.

Dramatic irony usually entails a situation which produces just the opposite result of what the participants had anticipated. When Rosencrantz and Guildenstern accompany Hamlet to England bearing orders for Hamlet's execution, it is ironic that the two courtiers meet with the very fate that had been intended for Hamlet. Likewise, when Eve succumbs to the serpent's entreaties because she has been promised God-like powers, it is ironic that she only succeeds in becoming mortal.

In David Lean's screen version of *The Bridge on the River Kwai* (1957), a British colonel (Alec Guinness) agrees to let his captured battalion construct a bridge for the Japanese because he feels the work will save their morale. It is ironic that he does manage to save their morale, but only by building a bridge that will obviously be used to transport enemy troops and munitions—but it is even more ironic that when the allied commandos arrive to destroy the bridge, which the colonel had hoped would stand for 600 years as a monument to British ingenuity and expertise, the colonel actually attempts to prevent its destruction!

Irony of fate, or as it is sometimes called "cosmic irony," operates on the assumption that fate is a force that actively intervenes in men's lives, almost always to their detriment. Although Oedipus is an overly proud and often arrogant man, he honestly attempts to avoid killing his father and marrying his mother. But Oedipus is a fated man, and no matter what he does he cannot elude his tragic destiny; in the course of the play, all the prophecies come true.

Vittorio De Sica's neo-realistic *The Bicycle Thief* (1948) appears to tacitly support the conventions of cosmic irony. A hopelessly poor Italian named Antonio has an opportunity to work as a bill-poster, but the job requires that he own a bicycle. After considerable sacrifice, he does manage to obtain the bicycle but, on the very day he starts his new job, the bicycle is stolen. His attempts to regain the bicycle fail and, driven to desperation, he steals another, and is subsequently caught and humiliated. Like Oedipus, Antonio's life appears to be fated, and it seems as though there is nothing he can do to elude that fate.

Another instance of irony that occurs in both literature and film which is worth mentioning is ironic point of view. Basically, ironic point of view refers to the discrepancy between what the characters say and do and what the writer or the film maker really means. This technique, which is usually used satirically, permits the artist to mock his creation without appearing to do so. For example, W. H. Auden's *The Unknown Citizen* is supposedly a tribute by the State to the ideal representative citizen, but the tribute reveals the anonymous JS/07/M/378 (the name of the citizen) to be a mindless conformist who has lived a totally vacuous and passive existence. Richard Attenborough's *Oh! What a Lovely War* utilizes ironic point of view throughout the film. When the British show girls, in an attempt to secure recruits from the audience, sing out, "We don't want to lose you, but we think you ought to go," it is patently obvious that the film's creators not only do not share their views, but are also mocking them.

Because it makes use of apparent contradiction and inconsistency, paradox is somewhat allied to irony. In Greek *paradoxos* means "incredible; conflicting with expectations." A paradox is a statement that appears not to make sense. In one of his *Holy Sonnets* John Donne says:

> Batter my heart, three-personed God: for You
> As yet but knock, breathe, shine, and seek to mend:
> That I may rise and stand, O'erthrow me . . .

When Donne requests that God overthrow him so he might rise and stand, he is employing a paradox. Literally, Donne's statement is self-contradictory, for to be overthrown is just the opposite of rising. The impact of Donne's paradox lies in its shock value: The apparent absurdity of his statement forces the reader to reconsider the line. The key to the meaning of Donne's paradox lies in the word "rise." If rise is understood in the sense of spiritual rather than physical ascension, then the line makes perfectly good sense. Donne asks of God that He overthrow his proud spirit so that he might attain the humility necessary for salvation.

A film which has baffled many reviewers and critics because of its extensive use of enigma and paradox is a collaborative effort by avant-garde novelist Alain Robbe-Grillet and director Alain Resnais entitled *Last Year at Marienbad* (1961). In his introduction to the text of the film[5], Robbe-Grillet suggests that the film's paradoxes are apparent rather than actual. By using an example of two people exchanging remarks, Robbe-Grillet argues that when people converse they actually exchange *views,* that is, they literally envision what they say. Hence, to Robbe-Grillet, there is no sharp line separating fantasy from reality, the image in the mind's eye is as real as the image of external reality. Thus, a sudden and seemingly paradoxical shift of place or the use of an enigmatic point of view are not paradoxes at all, but merely a reflection of the mind's alteration between inner and external realities.

Allusion is another means by which both writers and film makers are able to enrich and intensify their narratives. Basically, an allusion is an indirect reference to something that lies outside the work itself; most frequently, the allusion refers to a historical personage, event, or to some previous work of art. When the artist employs allusion, he allies his work to the emotions or ideas of another work. Although allusion represents a highly efficient method of communicating meaning, it is not entirely without risk. When he employs allusion, the artist assumes that his reader or his viewer has shared the same literary, historical or film experiences as he has. If the artist's assumption is correct, then a single line can greatly enlarge the resonance of his work; if, on the other hand, the allusion is too arcane or esoteric, then not only is the allusion lost on the reader or viewer, but it can easily confuse or disorient him as well.

As far as literature goes, most serious readers are familiar with the Bible and Shakespeare, and many with classical mythology as well. Thus, when William Blake, in *Song*, writes: "With sweet May dews my wings were wet/And Phoebus fir'd my vocal rage . . ." the reader recognizes that Phoebus is an allusion to Apollo, the Greek god of the sun. Or if a writer describes a character as being a "veritable Iago," the reader will immediately recall the diabolic evil of Othello's Ancient in Shakespeare's tragedy. On the other hand, few contemporary readers will recognize that a line in the drunken porter's speech in *Macbeth,* "Here's a farmer that hanged himself on the expectation of plenty" is an allusion to the abundant harvest of 1606 which was followed by a marked slump in the price of corn. Today, the same thing would be true if a writer referred to the Maharishi Mahesh Yogi: Most contemporary readers would be familiar with the one-time guru of the

Beatles, but ten, or even five years from now, another reader would most likely scratch his head in amazement.

For the writer, figurative use of language affords him the means by which he can state truths that a literal use of language cannot; the same, of course, applies equally to a film maker's use of his "figurative language" of images and sounds. A figure is not only a means of seeing the world in new and startling ways, but it can also involve us emotionally, make the abstract concrete, or condense, and thereby enrich, the narrative. By employing metaphor, simile, or personification, the artist can force us to make striking and unusual comparisons; or perhaps he aids us in seeing the commonplace in uncommon ways by his use of hyperbole or understatement. Because of its vividness, its richness, its density, figurative language represents an integral and substantial aspect of the narrative experience in both the film and in literature.

REFERENCES

1. Sarris, Andrew (ed.) *Interviews With Film Directors* (Bobbs-Merrill, New York, 1967), p. 309.

2. Lawson, John Howard, *Film: The Creative Process* (Hill and Wang, New York, 1967), p. 200.

3. Reisz, Karel, *The Technique of Film Editing* (Focal Press, New York, 1966), p. 238.

4. Sheridan, Marion C. *et al. The Motion Picture and the Teaching of English* (Appleton-Century-Crofts, New York, 1965), pp. 6–7.

5. Robbe-Grillet, Alain, *Last Year at Marienbad* (Grove Press Inc., New York, 1962), p. 13.

Peyton Farquhar is the name of the victim in Ambrose Bierce's short story, *Occurence at Owl Creek Bridge* which Robert Enrico made into a prize-winning short in 1961. Here, "Peyton" is feverishly trying to shake off his pursuers.

ANALYTICAL APPROACHES TO THE FILM:

CRITICISM

❝❝ The most important thing to remember
about film criticism is that it is not
fundamentally different from any other
kind of criticism.[1] ❞❞

JOHN SIMON

Here is a shot from what is probably the most famous surrealist film ever made, Salvador Dali and Luis Buñuel's *Un Chien Andalou* (1929). What is happening to the man on the bed? Why is he lying so rigidly still? If you are curious, you might want to see this film at a re-run house; if you are squeamish, take along a mask and a generous supply of. tranquillizers.

The Museum of Modern Art/Film Stills Archive

Despite her contemporary clothes, Monica Vitti appears hopelessly out-of-place in the industrial world of today. Here is a shot of her in a factory from Michelangelo Antonioni's *The Red Desert* (1963).

Courtesy of Audio Film Center/ Ideal Films

*Thou shalt love thy
neighbor as thyself . . .*
here is a shot of
the calm before the storm
in Norman McLaren's
Academy Award-winning
short, *Neighbors* (1952).

Courtesy of Contemporary
Films/McGraw-Hill

In this shot from Roman
Polanski's *Two Men
and a Wardrobe,* we see
the two men reacting
to the intolerance
and violence around
them by retreating
(or returning) to the sea
—still lugging their
wardrobe.

Courtesy of Contemporary
Films/McGraw-Hill

CRITICISM, a word mistakenly made synonymous with "finding fault," "making severe and adverse judgments," or "picking things apart," is essentially an act of evaluation. By relying upon his intelligence, experience, sensitivity and knowledge, the critic attempts to assess the artistic merits or deficiencies of a work of art. On the one hand, he serves society by calling attention to meritorious and excellent works and by denouncing the dishonest and the fraudulent; conversely, he serves the artist by responding to his work as an intelligent and sensitive member of his audience.

It is both necessary and important for the serious student of film to learn how to assess the film experience. In this country, unfortunately, the evaluation of films, for the most part, has been left in the hands of the film reviewer. The reviewer, usually a functionary of a newspaper or a periodical, too often possesses notoriously little knowledge of either the history of film or the principles of cinematography, and his assessment of a film is typically little more than a plot summary and a hasty evaluation—the evaluation commonly based on whether or not he thinks the "general" viewer will "like" the film. Thus, the film reviewer should not be confused with the film critic.

The film critic approaches the film as an art form; consequently, he distinguishes between films which are mere audio-visual diversions and films which possess artistic merit. Just as the literary critic feels no compulsion to evaluate all books, the film critic is under no obligation to assess or examine all films.

Ideally, the film critic should possess a variety of skills: He should be familiar with the history of film, its artistic and technological development; he should have a working knowledge of the principles of cinematography, as well as an undertanding of the techniques and conventions of dramaturgy—because film often draws upon other art forms, it is useful, if not imperative, for the critic also to be acquainted with literature and art history.

Although film criticism is in many ways allied to literary criticism, it has some singular features that set it apart from other art forms. First, film is characterized by movement: A film can never be arrested and scrutinized in the same manner as a novel, a painting, or a piece of sculpture. This is not to imply that the film critic can speak with any less acumen than other critics, but rather it means that the film critic must learn to utilize different skills. In addition, the film requires a special milieu: a darkened room, a projector and screen, and, of course, the film itself. This raises the most serious obstacle facing the serious student of film—accessibility.

Unless one happens to live in a major metropolitan area, the opportunity of viewing cinema classics on any kind of regular basis presents considerable difficulties. In some instances, many American classics are no longer even available. Out of the 200,000 films released in the United States since 1894, less than 20,000 are still extant.[2] For the interested student of cinema, the situation is not unlike a student of world literature finding himself unable to obtain a copy of *The Canterbury Tales, Don Quixote, Madame Bovary* or *Ulysses.*

Although the situation is dire, it is not hopeless. Nearly all colleges, universities or secondary schools, and some public libraries own 16 millimeter projectors and, in some instances, these institutions have managed to develop substantial film libraries. In those cases where the equipment is available but the films are not, it is possible to obtain the films from various leasing agencies at nominal fees.[3] The formation of a film society represents another method of gaining access to largely inaccessible classic and contemporary films. A less desirable, but alternate source for films is television. Although the substantially reduced image, the frequent obliteration of detail and poor light and color contrasts render television a less than ideal medium on which to view films, it does enable the film student to view works that might otherwise not be available. Thus, the raw materials of film criticism, the films themselves, are conceivably within the reach of everyone.

In approaching the film as a work of art, the critic is not only aware that the film differs from every other art in form, but he is also conscious that the film's realization and frequently its conception are unique. In most instances, works of art are both conceived and realized by a single intelligence. Film, of course, is different—it represents a collective or a communal art and often hundreds of different people will play a part of bringing a scenario to the screen. Even so, is true that the film is often dominated by the intelligence and personality of a single individual—the director.

The serious film student, of course, wants to determine who has contributed what to a given film. Usually he will consider the nature of the director's relationship to the completed film. Basically, two alternatives exist: The director can represent the hired technician who is responsible for supervising the actors and the cameraman, or he can be regarded as the creative individual who is most responsible for the character of the finished film.

At one point in the history of cinema, the director represented little more than the studio's flunky. The producer was the man who selected both the script and the leading actors, then assigned a director to the film. The director's responsibility was restricted to arranging the action for the cameraman to photograph and coaching the actors. The raw footage of the film was then assembled by the film editor.

In the early 1940's, the role of the director began to undergo significant changes. He began to acquire more control over the various phases of the film's creation. Although it was rare for him to have the last word on the final cut of the film—this privilege usually being reserved for the studio heads—the director was becoming a more complete film maker. In some instances, the director's role was not unlike that of an architect's—he both designed and supervised the creation of the film. Orson Welles, for example, not only directed *Citizen Kane* but he also co-wrote the film's screenplay.

In Europe, the attitude towards the director was somewhat more enlightened; it was taken for granted that the director was the creative intelligence behind the film. This attitude was finally articulated by French critic and film maker, François Truffaut, in an article entitled "La Politique des Auteurs," which appeared in the influential film journal *Les Cahiers du Cinema*. The complete film maker, according to Truffaut, was the *auteur*; for Truffaut, the *auteur* not only represents the film maker with complete artistic control but he is also the man with the personal vision, the film artist with both something to say and the artistic freedom to say it. As a consequence of the *auteur* theory, there has developed a tendency to consider directorial careers rather than individual films. Italian director Bernardo Bertoluccii described it this way:

> The filmmakers I love have made only one film. Godard started with *Breathless* and continued with the same film that proceeds along with his life. It's one film, even if it has many titles or many chapters. It's the same film and it walks along with him. To make film is a way of life. If we take out the title of the film and THE END and put the films all together, we will have the figure of one man, of an auteur, the life of an *auteur,* transferred in many characters naturally.[4]

Some of the film makers most frequently described as *auteurs* are Federico Fellini, Ingmar Bergman, Michelangelo Antonioni, Luis Buñuel, Robert Bresson, Jean Renoir, Alfred Hitchcock, Alain Resnais, Stanley Kubrick, and, of course, Truffaut himself.

It should be realized, however, that many films are not representative of the *auteur* theory—the director with complete control over his film is the exception rather than the rule. Thus, unless it is known for certain that the film is the work of an *auteur,* it is safer to assume that many points of view contributed to its final form. However, just because a film is not an *auteur* film does not mean that it is without artistic merit; it simply means that the critic must alter his approach in some respects. His primary responsibility, of course, is to work itself, but he will probably want to determine who is responsible for the diverse contributions to the film: who scripted it, who directed it, who photographed it, who provided the musical score and, finally, who edited it. Naturally, even though the critic recognizes that the *auteur* determines the final shape of a film, it is valuable for him to be aware of the separate individual contributors to the *auteur* film as well. Although the *auteur* does make it possible for the critics to assess the film much as he would a novel, he should guard against the tendency to romanticize the director. In the final analysis, it is the work itself, not its *auteur* which justifies our interest in the film. As D. H. Lawrence once observed, "trust the tale, not the teller."

To examine or evaluate a film, the serious film student has at his disposal two basic critical methods, the extrinsic and the intrinsic approaches. The critic who utilizes the extrinsic approach views the film as a sociological phenomenon; for the most part, he examines its sociological, moral, and philosophic assumptions. Often the extrinsic approach will make use of causal arguments which seek to "explain" the film or account for its origins. A critic might, for example, attempt to argue that the drastic post-World War Two conditions in Italy gave rise to the neo-realistic film (*Shoeshine* [1946], *The Bicycle Thief* [1948], *La Terra Trema* [1948]) of poor men at odds with the war-ravaged world around them. Unquestionably, the extrinsic approach is capable of rendering valuable insights but, by its very nature, it does not eliminate such vital artistic problems as analysis, description and evaluation.

The intrinsic approach, on the other hand, takes as its subject the analysis and interpretation of the work itself. While the intrinsic approach recognizes that the film, to some extent, mirrors the historical, moral and intellectual atmosphere of its day, it assumes that these considerations are of secondary importance. With the intrinsic approach, the critic's primary responsibility is to the film's artistry.

The remainder of the chapter will examine six possible critical approaches to the film. Two extrinsic approaches will be considered first—"Film and Society" and "Film and Ideas"; the explication of these two methods will be followed by a model essay which utilizes elements from both approaches. Following the essay, four intrinsic approaches will be outlined: "Imagery in Film," "Setting, Mood and Atmosphere in Film," "Style and Stylistics in Film," and "The Evaluation of a Film." Two additional model essays will be included to illustrate the intrinsic approach.

The six approaches outlined in this chapter do not pretend to exhaust the ways in which a film can be examined. In addition, the film student might want to consider the following possibilities: character analysis, film as it reflects a historical period, point of view, structure, and tone. Finally, no matter what approach he might decide to take, the critic should bear in mind that his *raison d'être* is the film itself; his analysis and commentary should shape themselves accordingly. The best film critics believe that their points of view are—somehow—less important than the film they are writing about.

Film and Society

The Film and Society approach, as mentioned earlier, assumes that the film is a sociological phenomenon. It views both the film maker and the audience as products of society's all-pervasive influences. Thus, advocates of this approach argue that a film, through its revelation of a society's social, economic and political institutions, can provide insights into the mentality of a particular era.

The basic assumption of this approach is that the film maker mirrors his times. Siegfried Kracauer, for example, made an extensive analysis of the psychological tendencies of the German films from 1920 to 1930; the thesis of his *From Caligari to Hitler* was that the prevailing attitudes which ultimately led to Germany's acceptance of Nazism are reflected in the films produced in this decade. On a similar basis, a writer might argue that the disillusionment with war, and the breakdown of traditional values have given rise to an extensive use of fantasy in the films of the 1950's and 1960's like *The Yellow Submarine* (1968) and the 1970 re-release of Walt Disney's 1940 masterpiece, *Fantasia*. In another vein, a writer might suggest that the basic optimism of the American people in the 1940's and early 1950's was reflected in the abundant musical comedies and the dramas with the conventional "happy ending," such as *Singin' in the Rain* (1952) and *Sabrina* (1953).

Rather than dealing with general tendencies in a culture, the writer may well wish to restrict himself to more limited topics. He may, for example, examine the role of the Black in American films. By selecting four or five representative films (say *Pinky* [1949] through *Porgy and Bess* [1956] to *Uptight* [1968]), he should be able to document the emergence of a somewhat more realistic view of the Black American. Similarly, a study of the films of a transitional decade could indicate changing attitudes towards the church, the military, sexuality and morality in general.

Sometimes the critic who utilizes the extrinsic approach will attempt to evaluate the film maker's influence on society. Undoubtedly the method is provocative, but it is also fraught with problems. The basic objection raised against this kind of approach is that there is no objective way of establishing a direct cause-and-effect-relationship between the viewing of a film and a subsequent change in audience behavior. How could a writer prove, for example, that Leni Riefenstahl's propagandistic films *Triumph of the Will* (1934) and *Olympia* (1938) actually helped foster the spirit of nationalistic pride that did much to unify Nazi Germany? Reams of parti-colored prose were generated when *Bonnie and Clyde* (1968) and *The Wild Bunch* (1969) were released. Many writers argued that these films not only had deleterious effects on the sensibilities of their audiences, but they also encouraged violence. Similarly, can new life styles actually be traced to films such as *Blow-Up* (1967) or *Easy Rider* (1969)? Is morality "undermined" by films such as *I Am Curious—Yellow* (1969)? It's a case of the chicken or the egg argument all over again: The film maker insists that he simply portrays what he sees, whereas the moralist is convinced that the film maker is out to sabotage the values underlying the culture. Thus, it can be seen that the attempt to assess the film maker's influence on society is at best of questionable value and, in this type of approach, the film is not viewed on the basis of its own merits, but rather as a propagandistic vehicle.

The critic who utilizes the Film and Society approach should keep in mind that his first responsibility is to the work itself. Even though a film contains historical or sociological inaccuracies, it can still be a superior work of art. He who attempts to evaluate history or a society solely on the basis of its representation in film is courting disaster. If the film he wishes to discuss deals with a particular era or historical event, the critic or the student should attempt to consult additional source materials such as histories, periodicals and learned journals. This additional research can only serve to strengthen the authority of his observations.

In a theme which employs the Film and Society approach, the writer should initially set forth the central idea which will govern his paper. The thesis sentence, "The characterization of the Negro in Victor Fleming's *Gone With the Wind* (1939) typifies the stereotyped portrayal of the Black in American Films" would suggest to the reader that the discussion would center on the misrepresentation of the Black American. The writer would then want to include any historical facts that are relevant to his thesis. The body of the theme would probably consist of evidence that substantiates the initial statement. His concluding remarks could conceivably take several positions: He might attempt to put the portrayal of the Black American into a perspective by pointing up what seemed relevant in the characterization and what is essentially false; he might show how the stereotyped portrayal of the Black provided insights into the values of a society; or, he could contrast *Gone With the Wind* to a current film that offers a more realistic portrayal of the Black experience.

Film and Ideas

Although every great film embodies ideas, it reveals them dramatically and in an indirect fashion. Sometimes it will be found that the film makes use of a single controlling idea: a philosophical assumption (the absurdity of existence) as in *Shoot the Piano Player* (1962); an economic premise (the rich exploit the poor) as in *They Shoot Horses, Don't They?* (1969); a psychological proposition (man is governed by largely unconscious motivations) as in *Psycho* (1960); or a moral belief (man is intrinsically good/evil) as in *The Treasure of the Sierra Madre* (1947).

A film's ideas can often be traced to a single individual's influence. Naturalism, for example, was largely based upon the investigations of Charles Darwin. Those writers and film makers who were influenced by Darwin's work depicted man as a being whose existence was largely shaped by heredity and environment. In American literature, Darwin's ideas found expression in Theodore Dreiser's *An American Tragedy* and *Sister Carrie,* Frank Norris' *McTeague,* and Stephen Crane's *Maggie: A Girl of the Streets.* Erich von Stroheim's *Greed* (1924) an adaptation of Norris' *McTeague,* and F. W. Murnau's *The Last Laugh* (1924) (before it received the American ending) represent two films which incorporate the principles of social Darwinism.

Similarly, the publication of Sigmund Freud's work significantly influenced the novels and the films of the twentieth century. In France, Salvador Dali and Luis Buñuel collaborated on the surrealistic fantasy *Un Chien Andalou* (1929). The films of Jean Cocteau *(Blood of a Poet* in 1932 and *Orpheus* in 1950), and Alain Resnais *(Hiroshima, Mon Amour* in 1959 and *Last Year at Marienbad* in 1961) represent, in many ways, a continuation of this same tradition. Obviously, the critic who is familiar with the discoveries of Sigmund Freud will have a decided advantage in discussing films which incorporated psychological ideas.

In considering a film's ideas, it is also difficult to ignore the writings of Karl Marx. The early films of Sergei Eisenstein and Vsevolvd Pudovkin, for example, celebrate the victory of the proletariat over its oppressors. More recently, the films of Pier Paolo Pasolini *(The Gospel According to St. Matthew* in 1964 and *Teorema* in 1969) tacitly support the assumptions of Marxist doctrine. For instance, in *Teorema,* the members of a wealthy industrialist family are depicted as empty and decadent; the factory workers, on the other hand, appear virile and righteously indignant at their exploitation. A writer, however, should guard against assuming that every film maker who examines economic exploitation is *ipso facto* a Marxist; more probably, he is simply a man who is troubled by the existence and perpetuation of injustice.

The ideas and assumptions of religion have influenced the arts from the beginning and film is certainly no exception. The life of Joan of

Arc was the inspiration for Carl Dreyer's *La Passion de Jeanne D'Arc* (1928), Victor Fleming's *Joan of Arc* (1948) and, more recently, Otto Preminger's *Saint Joan* (1957), and certainly many contemporary film makers (Robert Bresson, Federico Fellini, Ingmar Bergman and Luis Buñuel to name just a few) have examined the nature of man's relationship to, variously, the Roman Catholic Church and God.

There are several ways for the critic to assess what ideas are contained in a film. He might begin by examining what kind of role the environment plays in the film under consideration (Robert Flaherty's *Nanook of the North* [1922], and Pare Lorentz' *The River* [1937] are two obvious examples of environments occupying central positions in a film)—if the characters are constantly depicted in squalid and depressing environments, the writer should attempt to examine how their destinies are shaped or influenced by their surroundings. Depiction of character is certainly important: Who are the film's villains, its sympathetic characters, and why? If institutions (the church, education, the military) or their representatives appear in the film, how are they portrayed? What seems to be the film maker's attitude towards his subject? What kinds of metaphors and symbols does he make use of? What is the nature of reality in the film, i.e., could the film be described as realistic or fantastic?

Again, it cannot be overemphasized that although a study of a film's ideas can help to illuminate aspects of the film experience, the film possesses its own justification—it is not a substitute for philosophic, religious, political or economic doctrines.

In his theme on "Film and Ideas," the writer should state in his introductory remarks what he feels are the central ideas (or idea) of the film. The title "Existential Alienation in Antonioni's *Red Desert*" would obviously imply that the writer was going to examine the film in the light of the writings of the existential philosophers, specifically: Nietzsche, Heidegger, Jaspers, Sartre and Marcel. In the body of his paper, the aspirant critic would probably examine, in detail, those scenes which he felt best exemplified "existential alienation." His concluding remarks would be directed towards an evaluation of the idea and the function it served in the film. He might, for example, conclude that the presentation of the idea was persuasive and artistically well integrated, or he might argue that the idea intruded on the film's artistry.

The following critical model utilizes the extrinsic approach: it combines elements from both the "Film and Society" and the "Film and Ideas" approaches.

INTOLERANCE, VIOLENCE AND ABSURDITY IN ROMAN POLANSKI'S *Two Men and a Wardrobe*[5]

Implicit in Roman Polanski's award-winning short *Two Men and a Wardrobe* are the ideas of Charles Darwin and Sigmund Freud. Darwin's investigations of evolution and animal behavior had the effect of undermining the largely romantic notions of man's innate goodness. Subsequent research into man's origins has also revealed that man's instinct for violence and cruelty are at least as strong as his instinct for love and compassion. Freud's work, most of which was based on the assumption that man was often prey to largely unconscious influences, not only called into question the rationalistic philosophies of the 18th and 19th centuries, but also paved the way for surrealist and absurdist movements of the 20th century. Polanski's *Two Men and a Wardrobe* portrays society as intolerant, violent and absurd.

Zoologists, following the footsteps of Darwin, have demonstrated that, historically, societies of animals have been characterized by internal cooperation and external aggression. This trait is manifested in human society by a characteristic distrust of the outsider. In an interview, Polanski once remarked that *Two Men and a Wardrobe* was the only film he has made in which he "meant" something. Among other things, he wanted to show society's intolerance towards someone who differs from the norm.

From the start, Polanski's protagonists are set apart because of the immense wooden wardrobe they carry with them. By insisting on taking the wardrobe with them wherever they go, Polanski's two characters constantly experience rejection. They are, for example, denied admittance to a street car, turned away from a restaurant, later a hotel, shunned by an attractive young woman, and finally beaten up by a gang of young toughs. Polanski, of course, could have been using the wardrobe to fulfill some specific symbolic function, but it seems more likely that he is simply using the wardrobe as a means to set the two men apart from the remainder of society. Perhaps though the two men are carrying the "burden" of their very identities—or at least their individualities—about with them.

As in many of Polanski's other films, violence plays a dominant role in *Two Men and a Wardrobe*. The notion that civilization is no more than a thin veneer over man's animal violence is implied throughout. There are four examples of violence in the film, two of which directly affect the protagonists, and each successive incident is characterized by being more violent than its predecessor. The first portrays a group of idle young toughs who stone to death a harmless kitten. Afterward, they decide they will frighten a young girl with the cat's body, but are frustrated in their attempts when the two men inadvertently intervene, thus permitting the girl to escape. The toughs then proceed to beat up the two men for interfering with their "fun." Saddened and weary from their experiences in society, the two men attempt to rest in a stockyard of empty barrels, but are driven away by a watchman who beats them with a stick. The two men finally abandon the city. Leaving, they pass a wooded section of the city; out of sight of the two men, but in sight of the audience, the camera records with clinical detachment the agony of a man being beaten to death. Polanski's portrayal of violence suggests that it is an integral aspect of modern society.

The film reveals the unconscious absurdity and the irrationality of society primarily through its use of background. For example, when the two men are expelled from the restaurant, in the background a large dog is seated at the table of his master with a plate placed before him. At the adjoining table, a drunk is passed out in front of a wine bottle. The hotel inn-keeper apparently rejects the two men because of the awkward size of their wardrobe, but in the subsequent scene, he welcomes a family bearing an equivalent amount of normal-sized luggage. Finally when the men are driven from the stockyard of barrels, it is apparent that the barrels, at least in the eyes of the watchman, are deemed more valuable than they are.

In the end, the two men and their wardrobe come to the seashore, to return to the ocean from which they had emerged in the opening scene of the film. Inasmuch as the initial life forms evolved from the sea, the opening and closing scenes possess obvious Darwinian overtones. Polanski's conclusion to the film appears to suggest that the hostile environment of the sea is preferable to the narrow-minded, absurd cruelty of human society.

As was pointed out earlier in this chapter, the intrinsic approach concentrates on the analysis, description and evaluation of the film. The writer who makes use of it not only attempts to analyze "how" a film means, but also endeavors to evaluate the success of the film as an artistic creation.

Film and Imagery

A film is a sensuous experience. Whatever artistry it possesses is largely attributable to a successful juxtaposition of images and sounds; its imagery consists of pictures, or portions of pictures, and sounds. It is through pictures and sounds that the film maker is able to convey experience. Since images and sounds often possess connotations, a study of a film's imagery also includes its use of figurative language—the simile, metaphor, symbol, personification and allegory.

The power of a film's imagery is discernible in its ability to awaken the "sensory memory" of the viewer. Although the film experience is restricted to sights and sounds, it can be argued that the film is also capable of evoking olfactory and tactile responses. An extreme close-up of a coarse stone, for example, would have the effect of recalling to the viewer the tactile experience of a rough-textured surface. Similarly, a shot of a waterfront fish market could engender the pungent fish smells which usually permeate such a setting.

Since the critic assumes that every image and sound in a film is carefully chosen, he will not only want to determine what particular images and sounds have been selected, but also how they have been presented. Initially, the writer should attempt to distinguish between the film's significant and secondary images—obviously, some images are more important than others. There are several ways of identifying a film's important images and sounds: by observing how much time they are alloted, by watching for instances of repetition, and by analyzing what images and sounds accompany the film's crucial shots and scenes. For example, it might be observed that whenever a particular character is photographed, he always appears to be dwarfed by or encapsulated in something—a wall, a building, an automobile. Visually the film maker is suggesting that this person is trapped. Sometimes it will be found that the film maker will employ a "controlling image"; this is a term that is used to describe an image that has been developed so intensely and thoroughly that its influence pervades the entire film. The desert sands of David Lean's *Lawrence of Arabia* (1962) would represent an example of a controlling image.

As he examines the film's imagery, the critic will also want to analyze the film maker's use of sound. Is it excessive or restrained? Does he make use of silence? Does the sound support the image (synchronous) or oppose it (asynchronous)? When the film maker uses music, is it possible to identify his sources?—music of a particular period, for example, would tend to recall the characteristics of that era.

Imagery in a film is thus not only a means to enrich and intensify the film experience but also to convey a significant portion of the film's meaning. Thus, once the critic has established what he thinks are the basic imagistic patterns in the film, he will want to determine how the imagery conveys meaning. For example, the writer might notice that the film maker frequently interrupts the flow of the narrative to photograph objects as Antonioni did in *Blow Up*. It is then the task of the writer to determine the nature of the relationship that exists between the objects and the characters. What kinds of objects are they—modern, traditional, functional or decorative? A series of shots of modernistic objects composed of plastic or some sort of new metal alloy may be used to suggest that the characters are "plastic," that their values are moulded by the largely artifical milieu which surrounds them. Sound, too, of course, can be used as a metaphor or a symbol. An insistent mechanical rhythm could be used as a metaphor for a pervasive anxiety as in Joseph Mankewicz' *Suddenly Last Summer* (1960). Incoherent and barely audible dialogue, a literary technique perfected by James Joyce in *Ulysses* and T. S. Eliot in *The Wasteland,* may represent the artist's way of suggesting that communication has broken down between people. Mike Nichols in *The Graduate* (1968) uses this device to good effect.

In developing a theme on the imagery in a film, the writer will want to state what he feels are the dominant imagistic patterns of the film. In his introductory remarks he should indicate how the film maker's use of imagery augments our understanding of the work. The commentary that follows could be developed in several ways: by analyzing the source and nature of the imagery and relating this information to the film's theme or central idea; by demonstrating that the film's imagery emphasizes certain sensations and subordinates or eliminates others (a film, for example could emphasize sound or noise, but deemphasize sight by consistently using dark, shadowy, obscure and blurred images which might suggest that the character's ability to see or understand is impaired in some way); or by simply analyzing how the film maker's use of imagery helps to establish tone or shapes our attitudes and con-

clusions about the film as a whole. Concluding remarks should attempt
to assess the film's imagery. The writer might argue that the film maker's
use of imagery intensifies or enriches his experience, or he might indicate that the film's images appear contrived and feeble. Whatever form
his remarks may take, however, the writer must provide "evidence" to
support his conclusions.

Setting, Mood and Atmosphere in a Film

The film maker's choice of setting and what use he makes of it
is tremendously important, for it determines, to a large extent, the mood
and atmosphere of his film. Because a setting is often used metaphori-
cally or symbolically, it is somewhat related to imagery.

Setting is the locale of the film and includes any properties that are
present on the set. It is conceivable for a film maker to utilize only a
single setting during a film—a room, an open boat, the interior of an
airplane, but it is far more likely that many settings will be employed
because one of the most salient properties of films is that unlike a theatrical presentation, they can actually change locales. Movies move.

The film maker uses setting to achieve a variety of purposes and
effects. He might, for example, use it to impart a particular texture to
the film: realism, romanticism or fantasy. Setting also might be used
to structure a film; opening and closing on identical shots (a "frame"
device) or having the setting parallel the fortunes of a character, as in
the case of a journey, an ascension or a decline. For example, an east
to west journey paralleling the "birth" and "death" of the sun, might
culminate in death, or a family that lives in an expensive house on a
hill might experience a series of events which conclude with their moving
into a mean boardinghouse in the valley below. Finally, a setting can
be used as a metaphor or a symbol. The writer who attempts to analyze
a film from the vantage point of setting will certainly want to consider
all of these possibilities.

Some settings, of course, will be found to be more important than
others. Michelangelo Antonioni's *Zabriskie Point* (1970) derives its
title from a setting. Zabriskie Point is a barren, dusty, considerably
eroded section of Death Valley. In the film, Antonioni uses Zabriskie
Point as a metaphor for the barrenness and aridity of certain values in
American society. Although the film does make use of other settings, a

writer could utilize this particular one as a focal point for his commentary on the entire work.

What the critic needs to concern himself with is *how* the setting is revealed. A city, for instance, could be portrayed as a vital and exciting place to live, or the same city could be revealed as constraining, dirty and oppressive. The writer will want to consider which elements of the setting are emphasized and which aspects are neglected or ignored. He will also want to analyze the film maker's use of black and white or of color. If the film is in color, which colors predominate? Yellow, red and orange might be used, as in a painting, to suggest passion or gaiety; more somber colors—greys, blacks and purples would evoke more melancholy moods. How does the film maker utilize space? Could the settings be characterized as open and spacious or are they claustrophobic? Similarly, a film maker's use of lighting will influence the way we perceive a setting. Are the settings brightly lit or are they dark and shadowy?

The writer who studies the use of setting in a film assumes that the film maker's choice of setting is intimately related to the film's overall meaning. The thesis sentence, "The desert is a controlling metaphor in Antonioni's *Zabriskie Point*," indicates that the writer plans to examine a single setting in light of its metaphoric implications. As he develops his theme, he will probably touch upon the following topics: how the physical characteristics of the setting relate to the firm's overall theme; the way the use of setting controls atmosphere, mood and tone; and, finally, the nature of the relationship that exists between the setting and the characters. Thus, the body of the writer's theme will constantly indicate the relevance and suggestiveness of the film's setting. The writer's concluding remarks will probably take the form of an assessment of the appropriateness of the film maker's choice and handling of setting in the film.

Style and Stylistics in a Film

Style in a film refers to the film maker's manner of expression and the devices he employs in the film. A study of style would thus include presentation of images, use of sound, transitions (cuts, wipes, dissolves, etc.) color, rhythm, movement and figurative language.

It will be found that a unique film style is frequently identified with a particular film maker: The work of Antonioni, Fellini and Welles, for instance, is so idiosyncratic that their styles can be identified almost immediately. In some cases, the film's form can influence a style; for example, a film maker who utilizes a particular style for a satire or a fantasy will probably alter his style if he is called upon to do a documentary or a drama. A style that seems appropriate to its subject is described as *decorous,* whereas a style that calls attention to itself by its artificiality or its "flashiness" is deemed *manneristic.*

The writer who undertakes a study of a film's style is actually making a close study of the film's "language." In his analysis, he attempts to isolate and scrutinize those elements of a film which make it unique. Essentially, he is setting out to demonstrate that the film maker's style is inseparable from the film's meaning.

A study of style is probably the best way of ascertaining a film maker's control of his material.

Since the film is primarily a visual medium, the writer might begin his examination by analyzing the film's camera work. How are the images presented? Are they intimate, that is, does the film maker work close to his subject with close-ups and medium-close shots, or does he remain at a distance from his subject? How are we forced to perceive the images? Do we look up to them, look down on them, see them in sharply defined detail or through an impressionistic haze? What about the film's rhythm? How does it flow, slowly and langorously? with a steady inexorable rhythm? with a stacatto and breathless pace? What kinds of transitional devices does the film maker favor—cuts, wipes, dissolves, superimposures or fades? How does he approach his subject? Does he move in by a series of cuts? Does he "zoom" in? Does he track in? Are there any examples of unusual visual techniques— masks? split-screen? wipes?

After the writer has analyzed the film maker's visual style, he will want to consider the film maker's use of sound, point of view, use of black and white or color, lighting, and his use of figurative language. Does the film maker favor particular symbols or metaphors? Does he make extensive use of paradox?

Inasmuch as a study of style should represent a close and intensive analysis of a film, it may be profitable for a writer to isolate a single scene in a film and examine it in detail. If a writer elects this particular approach, he should make sure that the scene is representational, that it is characteristic of the film as a whole. In other words, what the writer says about this scene should also be generally applicable to the rest of the film.

The critic who analyzes stylistics might want to begin his theme with a descriptive statement of the film's style. He might, for example, characterize it as simple and unobstrusive, as inventive, or as ornate and idiosyncratic. If the writer feels that the style is particularly well suited to the narrative, he might want to include this observation in his initial remarks. Although the body of the critic's theme will probably represent a close analysis of the film's language, he can develop his central argument in several ways: the writer might concentrate on the appropriateness of the style to the film; he might restrict himself to a simple descriptive analysis of the style; or he might want to isolate stylistic characteristics that are unique to the film maker. The writer's concluding remarks will be based upon the research presented in the body of the theme. Depending upon his reasons for analyzing the film's style, his concluding remarks might either take the form of an evaluation or a summation.

STYLE IN MC LAREN'S *Neighbors*

Norman McLaren's Academy Award-winning short, *Neighbors* (1952) is essentially a contemporary morality tale based upon scripture from St. Matthew: "Thou shalt love thy neighbor as thyself." The parable, as a form, is not much in evidence in the contemporary film, but McLaren's highly stylized film technique makes *Neighbors* convincingly effective. McLaren utilizes a technique which he has called "pixillation." In an issue of *Canadian Film News,* McLaren described pixillation as a method of "applying the principles normally used in photographing of animated and cartoon movies to the shooting of actors: that is, instead of placing drawings, cartoons or puppets in front of the animation camera, we place real human beings."[6]

Like the parable, its literary counterpart, *Neighbors* is a highly unrealistic narrative; pixillation, because of its ability to dramatically exaggerate and distort movement, is well suited to this particular film. The technique, essentially an outgrowth of stop-action cinematography, enables McLaren's two protagonists to perform unusual feats: In the course of the film, they slide across the grass as though they were equipped with microscopic roller skates, dance in mid air, and erect wooden picket fences with a mere wave of their hand.

McLaren applies a sophisticated visual style to an essentially simple story line. Two neighbors, almost identical in appearance, are sitting in their front yards reading newspapers when a small flower suddenly springs up on their property boundaries. Unwilling to share the flower, both men claim ownership and soon come to blows. Eventually they destroy each other as well as the flower.

Initially, the film's style renders the two characters as comic: their movements and gestures possess a Chaplinesque quality that evokes laughter. However, comedy gives way to the macabre when the men begin to fight. Initially, the style had been employed to delineate the latent comedy in simple behavior, but now it is used to intensify and exaggerate the hideousness of violence.

The setting of *Neighbors,* in keeping with the narrative, is characterized by simplicity. The main setting is a grassy plot that could virtually be located anywhere. The only props employed are simple house fronts conspicuously propped up by sticks, two canvas lawn chairs and two newspapers. The spartan setting helps to emphasize the allegorical nature of the film.

Though the film employs no dialogue, it does make use of a rhythmically insistent electronic sound track. In the first third of the film, the electronic music comically underwrites the characters' actions. In the violent episodes, it is used to counterpoint ironically the brutality of the fight. The largely mechanistic rhythms of the score unite primitive violence and modern technology in a striking and unsual manner.

Like the literary parable, the use of symbolism and irony in *Neighbors* is unambiguous and straightforward. Ironically, the major symbol in the film, the flower, occasions the brutal fight between the two men. As if to suggest that beauty is plentiful, McLaren has two flowers spring up on the graves of the deceased neighbors and he adds an additional touch of irony by causing four fence slats, which a short time earlier had been used by the two men as swords and clubs to form crosses on the graves of the neighbors.

The non-realistic, largely experimental style of *Neighbors* seems well suited to the film, for it dramatically portrays violence as a simplistic and mechanical act. Although the theme and the story are familiar, the style sets *Neighbors* apart as an unusual example of a film parable.

Evaluation of a Film

For many reasons, the theme on evaluation is the most demanding of all critical pieces to write. It requires that the writer have sufficient viewing experience to be able to compare and contrast the film under consideration to other important or even great films. Considerable viewing experience will also enable the writer to evaluate the film's originality as well. In addition, the writer should have some understanding of the principles of cinematography in order to be able to assess the artistry of the film's visual accomplishments. Finally, he must be able to evaluate the emotional, philosophical and aesthetic dimensions of the film.

The critic might begin by attempting to evaluate his emotional and intellectual response to the film. He may have been struck, for example, by the intensity of the emotions the film aroused in him. He may have found himself moved by the film's lifelike vividness, the humanity of its characters. He experienced elation at the characters' triumphs, pity at their tragedies. In short, he found the film maker's imitation of life to be persuasive—it caused him to care. On the other hand, the writer might discover that he was more intellectually than emotionally involved in the film. Some films, by means of point of view, tone, or style seek to keep the audience at a distance from the action. Emotional involvement comes later, through reflection. Thus, a film does not necessarily have to overwhelm its audience emotionally.

The writer who is attempting to evaluate the film's artistic success will also want to evaluate the film's philosophical assumptions about the nature of reality. In his analysis, the writer has at his disposal two formidable weapons: his own experience of the world and his ability to reason. No matter what form a film might take, it is still subject to considerations of credibility and truthfulness. If a film portrays the world in terms of a neat dichotomy of good and evil its credibility diminishes, for we rarely observe people who can be lauded as all good or despised as wholly evil. On the other hand, a film can portray a vision that has no discoverable counterpart in reality but still be deemed truthful. Alain Resnais' *Last Year in Marienbad,* for example, shares only a passing acquaintance with reality as it is normally perceived, but as an exploration of an inner, subjective reality, the film is uncompromisingly honest.

In some instances, it might be found that the film proposes a solution to the philosophical issues that it raises. For example, a film might document the moral and intellectual corruption of a particular society and conclude by arguing that since the society is unresponsive to change, it must therefore be destroyed. A writer who is evaluating a film will surely want to assess this conclusion in light of what he knows. He would probably want to consider the truthfulness of the film's representation of the society, and he would certainly want to question the validity of the film's either/or conclusion.

When he turns his attention to a film's aesthetic character, the writer needs to consider many factors. Is the film beautiful?—that is, does it possess harmony, unity, symmetry and proportion? Could its theme be described as universal? Does it deal with important and perrenial problems of the human condition, or is it concerned with topical and secondary issues? Does the film possess richness and density of expression? Could it stand up to repeated viewings? The writer will also want to assess the film maker's control of his material, his choice of point of view and tone and certainly his use of figurative language.

A critic will always want to evaluate the film as an entity. Although it may possess flaws and imperfections, these should be placed in a perspective. If the film as a whole is characterized by power, originality and vitality, its flaws will constitute only minor imperfections.

The introduction of a theme on evaluation should state, in brief terms, the writer's assessment of the film as a whole. In the body of the paper, the writer will want to isolate and examine those elements of the film that led to his favorable or unfavorable evaluation of the film. Since the theme of evaluation always entails a judgment, it is imperative that the writer take a stand—he cannot remain neutral. If his arguments are cogent and well reasoned, the total effect of the theme should prove to be persuasive.

Occurrence at Owl Creek Bridge: AN EVALUATION

Robert Enrico's *Occurrence at Owl Creek Bridge* (1961) represents an excellent example of what can be accomplished by the short film narrative. Although the film shows great fidelity to its literary source, a short story of the same title by Ambrose Bierce, in many ways it improves upon its original.

The short story, for example, provides explicit motivation for the hanging, but Enrico simply presents us with a man who is about to be hanged. Consequently, the film attains a timelessness and a universality that were not present in the original. The film's protagonist, a Southern planter named Peyton Farquhar, becomes representative of all men who love life and yet are destined to die.

Enrico promotes the audience's identification with the condemned man by means of subtly shifting points of view. Initially, the camera is distant and detached from the proceedings on the bridge. But, almost immediately, the camera descends to the bridge in a langorously paced tracking shot which slowly, but inexorably, commits the audience to the hanging. Point of view then shifts from detached narration, to the viewpoint of a narrator-participant (the Union soldiers), to first-person narration (Farquhar himself), and finally to the interior monologue (the internalized escape fantasy). The shifts in point of view cause the audience to perceive and experience the hanging through the eyes of the condemned man.

The camera work throughout the film is economical yet richly suggestive. Frequent low camera angles of the Union soldiers, for example, render them as overpowering and authoritative; conversely, the condemned man is revealed as defenseless and frightened. Later in the film, Enrico makes suggestive use of a telephoto lens by using it to film the planter rushing towards his wife: Although he is running desperately, the lens causes him to appear to be getting nowhere.

With few exceptions, the sound track is dominated by sounds derived from nature. Inasmuch as the film is essentially an affirmation of life, Enrico's choice of sound seems singularly appropriate. In many instances, the sounds are slightly exaggerated in order to convey the condemned man's sensitivity to the life of which he is about to be deprived.

The film displays an inventive use of symbolism and irony. Enrico employs a striking visual metaphor when he has the Union sergeant remove the planter's pocket watch. Poised precariously over the waters of Owl Creek (water is a traditional life symbol) with a noose about his neck, the condemned man is being both figuratively and literally robbed of time.

The film's overall irony—the viewer's belief that he is witnessing the miraculous escape of a condemned man when he is actually watching an instant of time in the mind of a dying man—frames all the film's other ironies. During Farquhar's fanaticized escape, his senses become preternaturally keen and alert: He views the veins of a leaf, a spider spinning a web, the jewel-like qualities of a dew drop refracting light, and he pauses to smell the fragrance of a flower. Ironically, what had appeared to be a film about death actually turns out to be a film that celebrates the wonder of life and the basic instinctual drive for survival.

The most frequently voiced objection to the film is its conclusion. The film's detractors argue that it is contrived and deliberately deceives the viewer. A close examination of the film, however, will reveal that this is not at all the case—Enrico employs abundant aural and visual clues which suggest that the film has abandoned "objective" time in favor of "subjective" time.

Although there are at least four other indications of the alteration of time, the most obvious instance occurs just after Farquhar, who has fallen into Owl Creek when the hangman's rope broke, surfaces in the water beneath the bridge. The camera records the activities of the Union soldiers in slow motion and the sound track is slowed down, thereby suggesting that time is being retarded. Since the condemned man's fantasized escape actually takes place in a split second, Enrico's alteration of time seems both legitimate and appropriate.

Occurrence at Owl Creek Bridge represents a reaffirmation of the preciousness of a human life. Enrico's control of his medium gives us an unusual and perceptive insight into an aspect of human experience. Although the film does not represent a major contribution to film art, it is certainly an excellent example of the short narrative.

Unquestionably, there is at present a genuine need for quality film criticism. The fact that there is pitifully little important criticism being written today has obviously had an adverse effect on the artistic quality of today's films. Were more sensitive and intelligent criticism available, it might be possible to narrow the present gap that exists between the film maker and his audience. Upgrading both the quality and amount of film criticism could help to improve film accessibility by promoting the understanding and therefore the acceptance of the more intellectually challenging films.

Even though the changing attitudes towards the film as an art have been encouraging, it is apparent that even more radical changes will have to occur before the film can attain the artistic level for which it seems destined. Like any other art form, the film to a large extent is dependent upon the patronage of its audience. In a very real sense, *we* are responsible for both the achievements and the deficiencies of the film art . . . as well as for its future.

REFERENCES

1. Simon, John, *Private Screenings* (Macmillan, New York, 1967), p. 1.

2. These figures are based upon a brochure issued by the American Film Institute, 1707 H Street, N.W., Washington, D.C.

3. See appendix for a list of film distributors.

4. Gelmis, Joseph, *The Film Director As Superstar* (Doubleday & Company, New York, 1970), p. 117.

5. Each of the three films on which the model themes were based can be rented or purchased from Contemporary Films/McGraw Hill. *Two Men and a Wardrobe* (b&w, 15 min.); rental $25, purchase $250. *Neighbors* (col. 9 min.); rental $6. *Occurrence at Owl Creek Bridge* (b&w, 27 min.); rental $17.50, purchase $200. In the *East* write, Princeton Rd., Hightstown, N.J. 08520; *Midwest,* 828 Custer Ave., Evanston, Ill. 60202; *West,* 1714 Stockton St., San Francisco, Calif. 94133.

6. McLaren, Norman, "Pixillation," *Canadian Film News,* October, 1953, p. 3.

A GLOSSARY OF IMPORTANT FILM TERMS

AUDIO   Synonymous with sound and usually refers to the sound portion of the film.

BLIMP   A special housing which encases a camera used to record dialogue; the housing serves to soundproof the noise of the camera so it will not be picked up by the recording microphone.

CAMERA ANGLE   refers to the angle that exists between the camera and the subject; a "normal" angle corresponds to an eye level view; "low" angle is below eye level; "high" angle, of course, would be located above eye level.

CAMERA, MOTION PICTURE   Photographic instrument which makes a series of intermittent photographs on a strip of sensitized film which, when projected, produces the illusion of movement.

CAMERAMAN   Individual who operates the motion picture camera, or who contributes to its operation.

CLOSE-UP   A shot taken very close to a subject; if it were taken of a man, it would only show his head and shoulders.

CUT   The sudden transition from one shot to another produced by splicing separate shots of film together; with few exceptions, a cut is synomonous with a change in camera position.

and

"CUT!"   The command, usually uttered by the director, to stop the recording of a short; this order is given when the director is satisfied with the execution of the shot or scene.

DIRECTOR   Usually, the individual who is most responsible for the shape of the finished film; he supervises the action and the dialogue that occurs before the camera.

DISSOLVE   An optical effect whereby one shot gradually disappears as another simultaneously takes its place.

DOUBLE-EXPOSURE   The same strip of film is exposed on two different occasions; consequently, when the film is developed, two super-imposed images are visible.

DEVELOP, DEVELOPMENT   A chemical treatment of the exposed film so as to make the latent image—the invisible image registered on the film when the film has been exposed to light—visible.

DUB, DUBBING (sometimes called **lip-sync**)   Matching separately recorded sound to the lip movements of the actor on the screen. Dubbing can also be used to record musical scores.

EDITING   Splicing and assembling together the separate shots of the film in the proper continuity.
>   **CONTINUITY EDITING**   Portrays action in a "realistic" manner; the emphasis is on the creation of a continuous flow of events, apparently uninterrupted; the unities of space and time are fairly closely adhered to.
>   **DYNAMIC EDITING**   Fragments the action, and proceeds on the basis of juxtaposition and contrasts; the unities of time and space are frequently ignored.

EDITOR   The individual responsible for assembling shots and audio in proper continuity.

FADE   An optical effect whereby a shot gradually darkens to blackness—a **fade-out,** or lightens to reveal a new image—a **fade-in.**

FAST MOTION   The film moves through the camera at a slower than normal rate of speed; when film recorded in this fashion is projected, the action appears faster than normal.

FILM   A thin strip of celluloid or other transparent material with perforations along the sides that is coated with light sensitive emulsion and is capable of producing photographic images.

FINE CUT   An editorial stage in the film's development; the fine cut, a more completed version of the film, follows the rough cut; as the film moves towards its final form, excess footage is edited out.

FLIP   See **WIPE.**

FOOTAGE   The length of a film, measured in feet.

FRAME   An individual, transparent picture on a strip of film.

FREEZE FRAME   In the laboratory, a single frame is duplicated many times over. Thus, when the film is projected, the reproduced frame appears to stand still on the screen or to "freeze."

HIGH KEY A lighting technique that produces a brightly illuminated setting; often used in comedies and light dramas.

LOCATION Virtually any place, other than the studio or the stage, where the picture is being shot.

LOW KEY A lighting technique whereby the setting is deliberately under-illuminated in order to heighten dramatic action; often used in horror films.

MASK Strip of film which contains opaque portions that serve to exclude or reduce light transmission. Most commonly, masks are used for special effects and trick photography.

MIXING A process consisting of combining several sound tracks into a single sound track.

MONTAGE A cinematic method of representing reality that combines fragments of images and sounds from nature and then combines and juxtaposes them in such a way that they become something new; i.e., an image of an eye followed by an image of rushing water suggests tears. *Also,* montage is used to describe the impressionistic combination of brief shots that are used to supply a "time" or "mood" bridge in a film. A father searches the city for his son; the audience sees a brief shot of him talking to the policeman in the city park, another of him talking to the janitor at the school, and so on.

OPTICAL EFFECTS Dissolves, fades, wipes—in other words, any technique that utilizes the optical printer, which is a special mechanism that enables images from one film to be photographed onto another film by means of a special lens.

OUT OF SYNC The actor's lip movements are not in synchronization with the sound.

PAN Description of a camera movement; a pan is said to occur when the camera is held in a fixed position and rotated on a horizontal or vertical axis.

PRODUCER Individual who is responsible for the entire production of the film.

PROPS All the moveable fixtures, furnishings, materials and physical properties necessary for the setting.

RAW STOCK Unexposed or unprocessed film.

REEL(S)   The metal spools onto which the film is wound.

RETAKE   To redo a scene in which something has gone wrong—i.e., an actor muffing a line, a technician wandering on the set.

ROUGH CUT   An early editing stage in the film's development, usually the first time that the editor assembles the film from the selected takes.

SCENE   Usually a series of shots that are unified by time and space; in writing, a scene would be roughly analogous to a paragraph.

SCRIPT   The written blueprint for the film's production; in its initial form, the script is known as a **treatment**—a pre-production synopsis of the film; later it evolves into the **shooting script,** the final form of the script, which contains detailed and exact production instructions.

SEQUENCE   A division of the film, roughly analogous to a chapter in a novel; usually a series of events that are related by time, space or both.

SET   An artificial construction, including props, that is usually located in the studio, and simulates a locale—i.e., the main street of a small town.

SHOT   A single uninterrupted running of the camera (this may be actual or apparent).

SLOW MOTION   The film moves through the camera at a faster than normal rate of speed; when the film is projected the action takes place at a slower than normal rate of speed.

SOFT FOCUS   To film a subject slightly out-of-focus so that the image attains a kind of hazy quality; this technique is often used to make aging actors and actresses appear younger.

SOUND EFFECTS   Sounds which are added to the sound track in addition to the synchronized sounds of voices and music; most often sound effects represent off-camera noises.

SOUND TRACK   Either the thin band at the edge of the film that carries the sound, or a reference to the tape or optical sound track recorded separately from the visuals during the production.

SPLICE   To join end to end two separate strips of film so they make one continuous ribbon of film.

SPLIT-SCREEN, SPLIT-SCREEN MONTAGE   Two or more shots on the screen at the same time; if three different people were talking on the telephone from three different locations, the screen might be divided into three separate areas to enable the audience to view all three characters at once.

"SUPER," SUPERIMPOSE   A type of dissolve in which both images retain the same amount of light intensity.

SYNC, SYNCHRONIZATION   Term used to describe the proper coordination of sound and image.

TAKE   Each piece of action filmed before the camera, or to be filmed; for identification purposes, each piece of action is numbered by means of photographing a slate board which contains the necessary information.

TELEPHOTO LENS   Long optical camera lens which enables the cameraman to make close shots of action taking place at a considerable distance from the camera; this lens functions similarly to a telescope.

TILT   Description of a camera movement; a tilt is said to occur when the camera is moved up and down, either obliquely or vertically.

TITLE   Any written material which appears on the screen.

VOICE OVER   Any commentary or narration spoken over a scene by an off-camera individual.

WIDE-ANGLE LENS   A short-focus camera lens which gives a wider than normal field of view to an image.

WILD SOUND   Sound recorded separately from the filming. Often special sound effects are added later to the film's sound track.

WIPE   Optical effect. One shot changes to another by means of a moving line that travels from side to side, or top to bottom, etc.; as the line moves across the image it "pushes off" the original image and simultaneously reveals the new image. The **flip**, another optical effect, is very similar to the wipe except that in this instance the original image appears to "turn over" revealing another image on its reverse side.

ZOOM, ZOOMING   Accomplished with a special lens of variable and adjustable magnification called a zoom lens; this lens enables the cameraman to move from a wide-angle shot to a close shot and vice versa without changing the position of the camera.

SELECTED BIBLIOGRAPHY

- *Introductory Works on the Film Art*

    Bobker, Lee R., *Elements of Film,* Harcourt, Brace & World, New York, 1969.

    Huss, Roy and Silverstein, Norman. *Tthe Film Experience,* Dell Publishing Co., Inc., New York, 1968.

    Jacobs, Lewis, ed., *Introduction to the Art of the Movies,* The Noonday Press, New York, 1960.

    Lawson, John Howard, *Film: The Creative Process,* Hill and Wang, New York, 1967.

    Lindgren, Ernest. *The Art of the Film,* The Macmillan Company, New York, 1963.

    Mannogian, Haig P., *The Film-Maker's Art,* Basic Books, Inc., New York, 1966.

    Spottiswoode, Raymond, *Film and Its Techniques,* University of California Press, Berkeley and Los Angeles, 1951.

    Stephenson, Ralph and Debrix, J. R., *The Cinema as Art,* Penguin Books, Baltimore, 1969.

- *Film History*

    Brownlow, Kevin, *The Parade's Gone By . . . ,* Alfred Knopf, New York, 1968.

    Jacobs, Lewis, *The Rise of the American Film,* Teacher's College Press, Columbia University, 1939.

    Knight, Arthur, *The Liveliest Art,* New American Library, New York, 1957.

    MacGowan, Kenneth, *Behind the Screen,* The Dell Publishing Co., Inc., New York, 1965.

    Ramsaye, Terry, *A Million and One Nights,* Simon and Schuster, New York, 1964.

- *Film Theory*

    Arnheim, Rudolph, *Film as Art,* University of California Press, Berkeley and Los Angeles, 1957.

    Bazin, André, *What is Cinema?,* University of California Press, Berkeley and Los Angeles, 1967.

Eisenstein, Sergei, *Film Form,* Harcourt, Brace, New York, 1949.

———. *The Film Sense,* Harcourt, Brace, New York, 1949.

Kracauer, Siegfried, *From Caligari to Hitler,* Princeton University Press, 1947.

———. *Theory of Film,* Oxford University Press, London, 1960.

MacCann, Richard Dyer, ed., *Film: A Montage of Theories,* E. P. Dutton & Co., Inc., New York, 1966.

Pudovkin, V. I., *Film Technique and Film Acting,* Vision: Mayflower, London, 1958.

Reisz, Karel, *The Technique of Film Editing,* Focal Press, London, 1958.

• *Film Criticism*

Agee, James, *Agee on Film: Reviews and Comments,* Beacon Press, Boston, 1964.

Kael, Pauline, *I Lost It At The Movies,* Bantam Books, New York, 1965.

———. *Kiss Kiss Bang Bang,* Bantam Books, New York, 1965.

Kauffmann, Stanley, *A World On Film,* Dell Publishing Co., New York, 1966.

Rhode, Eric, *Tower of Babel: Speculations on the Cinema,* Chilton Books, Philadelphia, 1966.

Simon, John, *Private Screenings,* The Macmillan Company, New York, 1967.

Sontag, Susan, *Against Interpretation and Other Essays,* Dell Publishing Co., Inc., New York, 1966.

Taylor, John Russell, *Cinema Eye, Cinema Ear,* Hill and Wang, New York, 1964.

• *Film Scripts*

Agee, James, *Agee on Film: Five Film Scripts* (includes *The African Queen* and *The Night of the Hunter*), Beacon, Boston, 1958.

Antonioni, Michelangelo, *Screenplays of Michelangelo Antonioni: Il Grido, L'Avventura, La Notte, L'Eclisse,* Orion Press, New York, 1963.

Bergman, Ingmar, *Four Screenplays of Ingmar Bergman: Smiles of a Summer Night, The Seventh Seal, Wild Strawberries, The Magician,* Simon and Schuster, New York, 1960.

———. *Three Films by Ingmar Bergman: Through A Glass Darkly, Winter Light, The Silence,* Grove Press, New York, 1967.

Buñuel, Luis, *L'Age d'Or* and *Un Chien Andalou,* Simon and Schuster, New York, 1968.

Carné, Marcel, *Children of Paradise,* Simon and Schuster, New York, 1968.

DeSica, Vittorio, *The Bicycle Thief,* Simon and Schuster, New York, 1968.

Duras, Marguerite, *Hiroshima, Mon Amour,* Grove Press, New York, 1961.

Eisenstein, Sergei, *Potemkin,* Simon and Schuster, New York, 1968.

Fielding, Henry, *Tom Jones* (screenplay by John Osborne), Grove Press, New York, 1964.

Fellini, Federico, *Fellini's Satyricon,* Ballantine Books, New York, 1970.

Fonda, Peter, Hooper, Dennis, and Southern, Terry, *Easy Rider,* New American Library, New York, 1969.

Godard, Jean-Luc, *Alphaville,* Simon and Schuster, New York, 1968.

Kurosawa, Akira, *Rashomon*, Grove Press, New York, 1969.

McCoy, Horace, *They Shoot Horses, Don't They?* (screenplay by Robert E. Thompson), Avon, New York, 1969.

Renoir, Jean, *Grand Illusion,* Simon and Schuster, New York, 1968.

———. *Rules of the Game,* Simon and Schuster, New York, 1970.

Robbe-Grillet, Alain, *Last Year at Marienbad,* Grove Press, New York, 1962.

Truffaut, François, *Jules and Jim,* Simon and Schuster, New York, 1968.

- *Film and Other Arts*

Bluestone, George, *Novels into Film,* University of California Press, Berkeley and Los Angeles, 1957.

Nicoll, Allardyce, *Film and Theater,* Crowell, New York, 1936.

Richardson, Robert, *Literature and Film,* Indiana University Press, Bloomington, 1969.

Sheridan, Marion C., et al., *The Motion Picture and the Teaching of English* Appleton-Century-Crofts, New York, 1965.

- *Interviews with Film Makers*

Gelmis, Joseph, ed., *The Film Director As Superstar,* Doubleday & Company, Inc., Garden City, 1970.

Sarris, Andrew, ed., *Interviews with Film Directors,* The Bobbs-Merrill Company, Inc., New York, 1967.

PERIODICALS

- *Film Culture*
  G.P.O. Box 1499
  New York, N.Y. 10001
- *Film Heritage*
  Box 42 University of Dayton
  Dayton, Ohio 45409
- *Films in Review*
  31 Union Square
  New York, New York 10003
- *Film News*
  250 West 57th Street
  New York, New York, 10019
- *Film Quarterly*
  University of California Press
  Berkeley, California 94720
- *Media and Methods*
  134 North 13th Street
  Philadelphia, Pennsylvania 19107
- *Sight and Sound*
  British Film Institute
  81 Dean Street
  London W. 1, England
- *Take One*
  Unicorn Publishers
  P.O. Box 1788 Station B
  Montreal 2, P.Q., Canada

MAJOR DISTRIBUTORS FOR 16MM FILMS

- Association Films
  600 Madison Ave.
  New York, N.Y. 10022

- Audio Film Center
  34 Macquesten Parkway South
  Mount Vernon, N.Y. 10550

  Midwest
  2138 East 75th St.
  Chicago, Illinois 60649

  West
  406 Clement St.
  San Francisco, Calif. 94118

- Brandon Films
  221 West 57th St.
  New York, N.Y. 10019

  Midwest
  Film Center, Inc.
  20 East Huron St.
  Chicago, Illinois 60611

  West
  Western Cinema Guild, Inc.
  224 Kearny St.
  San Francisco, Calif. 94108

- Canyon Cinema Cooperative
  756 Union St.
  San Francisco, Calif. 94101

- Cinema 16
53 East 11th St.
New York, N.Y. 10003

- Columbia Cinematheque
711 Fifth Ave.
New York, N.Y. 10022

- Contemporary Films/
McGraw Hill
Princeton Rd.
Hightstown, N.J. 08520

    Midwest
    828 Custer Ave.
    Evanston, Illinois 60202

    West
    1714 Stockton St.
    San Francisco, Calif. 94133

- Continental 16, Inc.
241 East 34th St.
New York, N.Y. 10016

- Encyclopaedia Britannica
Education Corporation
425 North Michigan Ave.
Chicago, Illinois 60611

- Films Incorporated
1144 Wilmette Ave.
Wilmette, Illinois 60091

- Grove Press Film Division
80 University Place
New York, N.Y. 10003

- Institutional Cinema Service
20 East 10 St.
New York, N.Y. 10003

    Midwest
    203 North Wabash Ave.
    Chicago, Illinois 60601

    West
    2323 Van Ness Ave.
    San Francisco, Calif. 94109

- International Film Bureau Inc.
332 South Michigan Ave.
Chicago, Illinois 60604

- Janus Film Library
24 West 58 St.
New York, N.Y. 10019

- Museum of Modern Art Film Library
11 West 53 St.
New York, N.Y. 10019

- Radim Films
220 West 42nd St.
New York, N.Y. 10036

- Rembrandt Film Library
267 West 25 St.
New York, N.Y. 10001

- Roa's Films
1696 North Astor St.
Milwaukee, Wisconsin 53202

- United Artists 16
729 Seventh Ave.
New York, N.Y. 10019

- United World Films
221 Park Avenue South
New York, N.Y. 10003

    Midwest
    542 South Dearborn
    Chicago, Illinois 60605

    West
    1025 North Highland Ave.
    Los Angeles, Calif. 90038